DEFINITIONS

endless: 1. having no end, as a circle or chain. 2. of eternal duration, ceaseless, without pause. 3. never stopping.

falling: 1. to descend low or deep. 2. to drop by force of an irresistible influence (such as gravity or beauty). 3. to plunge lower than surrounding objects.

love: 1. selfless, other-centered passion. 2. chosen devotion to the well-being and happiness of others above self. 3. a score of zero (as in tennis). 4. to hold one's self in a zero position due to higher value placed on someone else.

AN ENDLESS FALLING in LOVE

TY GIBSON

Pacific Press® Publishing Association

Nampa, Idaho
Oshawa, Ontario, Canada

Author info: Ty Gibson • PO Box 338, Malo, WA 99150
email: tygibson@starband.net • website: www.lbm.org

Graphic design by MCM Design Studio, LLC.

Copyright © 2003 by Pacific Press Publishing Association
All rights reserved
Printed in the United States of America

All Scripture quotations are from the
New King James Version unless otherwise noted.
KJV indicates the *King James Version*.
BAS indicates the *Basic English Bible*.
TEV indicates *Today's English Version*.
NEB indicates the *New English Bible*.
TM indicates *The Message*.
AB indicates *The Amplified Bible*.
NASB indicates the *New American Standard Bible*.
RSV indicates the *Revised Standard Version*.
NCV indicates the *New Century Version*.
Phi indicates *J. B. Phillips*.
GW indicates *God's Word*.
NIV indicates the *New International Version*.
Mof indicates *Moffatt's*.

All emphases and words in brackets within quotations are added by
the author, except in quotations from *The Amplified Bible*.

Names and details in stories have been changed to
honor the privacy of the individuals involved.

ISBN: 0-8163-1979-0

03 04 05 06 • 4 3 2 1

CONTENTS

For James Rafferty

After 20 years of friendship and co-leadership with you,

I can honestly say I still like almost everything about you.

The greater marvel is that you still like me at all.

That you have been able to work so long with such a type A, perfectionistic,

hyper guy is a testimony to your character.

You are "an Israelite indeed in whom there is no guile."

This book is dedicated to you.

Every page is informed by your friendship.

WRITER'S PRAYER

Oh God, omnipotent and lowly,
   Descend to take this mind in hand;
Shape my thoughts to Your own,
   Til final line is writ to stand.

What of worth can any man tell,
   When subject sublime is You?
Dark the words are sure to be,
   Lest You tell first and You tell through.

Heart of God, beat strong in me,
   Pulsing deep to sense and know;
Let me to my reader speak,
   Your thoughts and feelings clear to show.

TIME TO FALL IN LOVE

As I passed by again,
I saw that the time had come
For you to fall in love.
I covered your naked body with My coat
And promised to love you.
Yes, I made a marriage covenant with you,
And you became Mine."
This is what the Sovereign Lord says.

Ezekiel 16:8, TEV

— *Chapter One* —

Remember and Imagine
ETERNAL LIFE

Awake my soul to daylight dreams,
To life's best moments sweet;
Amid the darkness so surreal,
Yet not at all discreet.

Faintly whispers in my ear,
All love I've ever known:
"Tis deeper love divine you feel
In all these moments shown."

WHY WOULD ANYONE want to live forever? Not me! I'm trying to work up the courage to end my life."

I met Egita in Latvia, that beautiful country on the Baltic Sea of near-fabled charm. Theirs is a culture rich in happy stories and peace-loving values. But at this present, long moment, they seemed frozen in time, living in the aftermath of a very tragic recent history. Taken over by the Soviet military, these lovely people were severely abused and ruthlessly dominated by their invaders. Many became atheists rather than struggling to fit the concept of a good God into their nightmarish existence. Egita was one of the unbelievers, or she was trying to be. With no motive to find relief from the dark images haunting her soul, she was attending a series of public lectures for which I was the featured speaker, probably to be entertained by the novelty of an American visitor.

While the idea of "living forever" was not the topic of my presentation that particular evening, I did use the term "eternal life" in passing. Apparently, as soon as I spoke those charged words, Egita was so repulsed by the notion that she heard nothing else I had to say. As she sat there about three rows back on the right, I couldn't help but notice her visible signs of discomfort. As soon as the meeting was over, she made her way through the crowd to the front. Thinking about some imaginary God doing us the supposed favor of giving us eternal life, her frustration intensified to the point that she simply had to tell me how totally repugnant the prospect was to her. In one hyper breath, Egita blurted out her tragic story:

"The Soviet soldiers came into our home. First, they shot my father in the head. Then they raped me and my mother and forced my brothers and my fiancé to watch, then killed them as well. My mother and I were commanded to pile on the front lawn everything of legal and sentimental value—my parents' marriage license, birth certificates, financial records and family photos. All of it was burned. Mama was taken away, and I have never seen her since that day."

The pain in this woman's eyes was more than I could bear to look into without lowering my eyes to the floor for relief. I could feel tears building inside me.

"Life is nothing but suffering," she continued. "I have no desire to live even another day. Living forever is a torturous idea."

As Egita spoke, it dawned on me that she was assuming eternal life would be just more of the same—more brutality and heartache, more insanity and pain. Life as she had known it was not worth living. So eternal life, she reasoned, would only make the burden of life inescapable.

"It's a ridiculous notion anyway," she said, turning to walk away. "I don't believe in God, so He can keep His eternal life. I don't want it."

This was no true atheist.

"I don't believe in God, so He can keep His eternal life"?

In that one sentence, this broken woman denied God's existence and then addressed His offer of eternal life as though He did exist.

"Egita," I spoke cautiously, as she bolted for the door, "would you please give me a chance to explain?"

She looked back at me with eyes that belied her hard exterior. I saw desire mingled with agony in her countenance, and I determined to make an attempt at probing past the hurt to arouse her latent longing for the God she could not wholly deny.

"What can you possibly say that would make any difference?" She began to soften.

"I think what I have to say could make a major difference, but you'll have to cooperate for a moment and do something a little awkward, and perhaps difficult."

"What?" she nervously inquired.

"Close your eyes."

Understandably, she hesitated.

"Please, Egita," I gently persisted, "close your eyes."

She cooperated.

"Now I want you to remember the very happiest moments of your life. Recall the people who have made you laugh with wonder and cry with joy, and your interactions with them."

I paused in silence and intently watched those hard features begin to melt away. A slight smile came to her lips and tears began to trickle down her cheeks.

As Egita opened her eyes, I asked, "What did you remember?"

She shyly told of special family outings on the lakeshore near her childhood home.

"It was so fun when Papa would put me securely on his back and swim far out in the water pretending to be a whale."

Her voice was nearly musical when she said, "Papa."

She told of times when her mother would talk and giggle with her late into the night.

"Mama loved me, and I always knew it. She was so beautiful and kind."

Then Egita's voice began to crack with emotion as she called to mind the unparalleled joy of falling in love. She described the young man who had captured her heart as her best friend in the entire world, extolling certain of his virtues and bragging of his charm.

"Falling in love with Edgar was the happiest and most wonderful experience I have ever known. Being loved by him and loving him in return was all I wanted to do with my life."

"Exactly," I commented.

With those memories fresh before her mind's eye, I began to explain the meaning of eternal life.

"Egita, now that you have remembered the best experiences of your life, you are prepared to imagine what eternal life will be like. Eternal life, Egita, will be like the immortalizing of those happy moments, like living forever in such moments. Eternal life will be like loving your papa and being loved by him. Loving your mama and being loved by her. And especially, Egita, eternal life will be like falling in love forever, nonstop, with your very best friend."

At first she looked more confused than enlightened. But with some prolonged discussion, Egita began to look like people do when they wake from a bad dream and realize it isn't happening. Shaking her head in her hands, she groped with her heart toward the light that was now penetrating through her pain.

Taking a deep breath, she asked, "What do you mean?"

"Egita," I further explained, "eternal life is an endless falling in love with the most beautiful and virtuous person in the entire universe . . . with God.

All the love you have ever tasted in this life had its origin in His infinite heart of love. Spending eternity with Him will be a ceaseless, ever-deepening love relationship of extreme happiness."

Egita smiled a second time, ever so slightly.

While there were some serious issues we had to work through regarding God's whereabouts during the tragedy that befell her family, she kept attending my seminar and I had the privilege of watching her fall in love with God. For this woman, eternal life had begun in the here and now.

Have you ever noticed that Jesus spoke of eternal life in just such terms?

"This is eternal life, that they may know You, the only true God, and Jesus Christ whom You have sent" (John 17:3).

Fascinating choice of words, don't you think?

The Savior did not define eternal life in terms of its *duration*, as if to say, "Eternal life is to live forever, millions and billions of years without end." Rather, He defined eternal life in terms of its *quality*. Eternal life, He explained, is a quality of living that derives its core essence from knowing God.

But what does Jesus mean in concrete, practical language? What shall we *know* when we *know* God, and how will that knowing shape the quality of our living?

"God is love, and he who abides in love abides in God, and God in him" (1 John 4:16).

It stands to reason that those who know God will know Him as He is.

One cannot swim in the ocean without getting wet, for the ocean is water.

One cannot bathe in the sunlight without being warmed by its rays, for the sun is fire.

One cannot know God without getting drenched in His love and warmed by its light, for God is love. To know God is to experience Him as a relational Person of perfect love, which is to know Him for who and what He is. If, as Scripture testifies, "God is love," then to live eternally with Him will be a continually deepening journey into the wonder and bliss of His love.

This is exactly what Jesus had in mind when He said, "Eternal life is to know God." Notice His own explanation:

"I in them, and You in Me; that they may be made perfect in one, . . .

Father, I desire that they also whom You gave Me may be with Me where I am . . . for You loved Me before the foundation of the world. O righteous Father! The world has not known You, but I have known You; and these have known that You sent Me. And I have declared to them Your name [the truth of Your character], and will declare it, that the [very same] love with which You loved Me may be in them, and I in them" (John 17:23-26).

Wow!

What a phenomenal revelation of the true meaning of life! Don't miss the significance of what Jesus is saying here. Let this penetrating glance into God's real purpose for your life totally impact and alter your thoughts and emotions.

First, notice that Jesus speaks in terms of His "desire." Here is a God of deep and flaming passion. Your eternal salvation and mine is not the stoic undertaking of a God of stern duty. Jesus does not pray, "Father, spare their wretched lives, for this is, unavoidably, the right thing to do. Perhaps we can shove them off into some remote corner of the universe."

No!

But rather, listen again: "Father, I *desire* that they be *with* Me."

He longs for our presence near Him, now and forever.

Oh God of intense desire,
Ignite in me the same passion
That burns in Your heart,
That I may as deeply desire to be with You!

Pause now to consider *why* Jesus desires us to be with Him. He speaks, no doubt in hushed tones of heartfelt realization, of the love He and the Father have shared in eternal ages past: "You loved Me before the foundation of the world." But then He agonizes over the fact that we are oblivious to that incredible love. We do not "know" the Father, He laments. Our fall into sin was, in fact, a falling out of God's love. So Jesus meets us at the specific area of our need. He has "declared" the beauty of God's character to our darkened eyes and deaf ears. And this He has done with a solitary purpose in mind: to draw us into the intimate circle of love that flows and surges between Himself and the Father. He yearns with deep desire that we, yes, you and me, would forever live in the pleasurable current of God's glorious love. His ultimate objective as our Savior is clearly stated: "That the love with which You loved Me may be in them, and I in them."

Let those words of divine intent take your breath away.

Finally, call your attention to the idea of *oneness* in the words of Jesus. Eternal life, He stated, is to know God. He then goes on to frame that experience in terms of becoming completely one with the Son in the oneness He shares with the Father: "I in them and You in Me, that they may be made perfect in one."

What does He mean by this?

When Jesus defined the qualitative essence of eternal life, He chose to employ perhaps the most intimate word in Scripture. "Eternal life," He explained, is to *"know"* God, which is the biblical word for sexual intimacy (Genesis 4:1), used by Jesus as a symbol of spiritual intimacy with God. He didn't say eternal life is to analyze God, or intellectualize about God, or acquire and systematize facts concerning God, or conduct ceremonies for God. He didn't say eternal life is to live forever in mansions of plenty and walk streets of gold. Jesus had something far more personal and profound in mind. To "know" God is to become experientially immersed in the reality of His "love," which, according to Jesus, involves becoming "one" with God.

As we shall discover in the pages that follow, God made us for intimate union with Himself, an intimacy that is best understood when paralleled to the closest relationship we know as human beings, that of marriage. For now, I'd like you to prepare yourself for the remainder of our journey together by doing what Egita did. Close your eyes and remember the happiest moments of your life. Recall the people who made you laugh with wonder and cry with joy. Especially remember, or imagine if you must, what it is like to fall in love. Those thoughts and feelings, ever so sweet, are but a slight taste of eternal life.

— *Chapter Two* —

Ancient Love
TRINITY

Alluring silhouette,
No features I see,
Til through the veil,
I pass to Thee!

ALL OF CREATION and all of biblical revelation comprise a sheer veil hanging provocatively before our eyes, alluring our hearts to behold a single mysterious form behind.

A physical form?

Yes—and more.

It is the shape of reality itself, taking its shape from the heart of its Designer.

This one mystery, which I will soon enough name, is the womb of all beauty. It is the absolute truth behind all that is true. It is the great river of goodness from whence flows all that is truly good.

If we draw the veil aside, step behind its folds, and peer into this wonder of all wonders, what shall we see? Dancing before our eyes in countless movements, we will behold one paramount reality . . . a single mystery that demystifies every other mystery and remains a mystery itself.

Love!

Were you hoping for something more, or something different? There is nothing that could truly be called more, for all else is less. And all that is different is quickly passing away like a bad dream. (So now would be a really good time to wake up!)

But what, exactly, is this thing we call "love"?

At its inner core love is not simply a law of nature, though it is the spring of all law. It is not a mere force of the cosmos, though it is the reservoir from which flows all life-giving energy. Nor is it the fragmented pieces of human goodness merging toward an eventual "collective consciousness," though it is the source of all genuine human goodness.

No!

It is more, far more, this thing we call love. It is the very personal character of a very personal God, who is Himself the matrix of all personhood. Love is the divine identity. It is who and what and how God is. It is the thought, the feeling, the motive, the power, the purpose, the impulse and the will of God. "God [the Person] is love" (1 John 4:8). The equation does not hold true in reverse. Love (as a depersonalized force) is not God.

But let's look a little deeper.

The Bible calls God "the Ancient of Days" (Daniel 7:9). To say God has been around for a long time would be a gross understatement. To say He's very old might conjure up the idea of "elderly." We might say God is anciently young—having always existed but having never aged. To the question, "How ancient?" the Bible answers, "He is before all things" (Colossians 1:17). "All things were made through Him, and without Him nothing was made that was made" (John 1:3). These Scriptures present two basic categories: (1) all things made, and (2) the unmade God who existed before all things made. Everything except God had a point of beginning. There was a time when freestanding, conscious life came into being, which means there had to be a time when no creature existed.

It staggers the mind to think of how long God existed as the "Ancient of Days" before venturing into the Creation quest. *Infinity* is the only word that comes to mind. We cannot comprehend it. We have only the bare idea itself, but absolutely no conceptual framework or even vocabulary to explain what it means. So we won't even try. But there is a significant question we may ask and answer to our profit. We can't help but wonder, *What was God doing before engaging in Creation?*

Think of it. He did exist. He was there, wherever *there* was. So what was He doing? How did "the Ancient of Days" spend those infinitely numerous ancient days "before all things"? In order to answer this question, we will listen first to God the Father and then to God the Son. They are, of course, the only Ones who can tell us.

Consider an inspired record that hints of God's pre-Creation activities—in my opinion one of the most astounding revelations of the divine character ever given to the human race. We find ourselves listening in on a faraway heart-cry spilling forth from the lips of God the Father, long, long ago:

"'Awake, O sword, against My Shepherd, against the Man who is My Companion,' says the Lord of hosts" (Zechariah 13:7).

Zechariah heard this tempestuous proclamation resounding through the prophetic heavens centuries before the incarnation of Christ. It reveals the cringing pain of God the Father as He contemplated the separation that would occur between Himself and His Son in order to save fallen humanity. He pondered the agony that would, like a piercing sword, plunge and twist deep within the sinless heart of Jesus and reach His own heart with sympathetic vibration.

But what else do you see here?

Take special notice of how God the Father speaks of God the Son, and you will find yourself standing before a crystal clear window into the divine heart. As you look, you will begin to understand what God is really all about. The true meaning of His love will emerge before your mind's eye. Referring to the condescending Messiah, the Father chose a Hebrew word with extremely intimate connotations: "the Man who is My *Companion.*" The word is '*amith*, and is translated in the New International Version, "the Man who is *close to Me.*" The New Century Version says, "The Man who is *My Friend.*" My own paraphrase is not at all a stretch from the intended meaning of the text: "the One who is *My closest Friend.*"

That's who the co-eternal Father and Son are to one another. They are, along with the Holy Spirit, the most intimate of friends. In this prophecy the Bible has given us a beautiful insight into God's love in its most ancient form.

But what makes this love what it is, and what it always has been in all ancient days past? What is its anatomy? Its secret of being? The answer lies in what we might call the reality of "otherness," the eternal truth of the "self" in the mutually conscious presence of the "other."

Take this in deeply.

God is three distinct persons who are one. "For there are three that bear record in Heaven: the Father, the Word, and the Holy Spirit; and these three are one" (1 John 5:7). They are three individual persons, each one existing as a separate, conscious self—Father, Son and Holy Spirit. And yet, according to biblical revelation, they are one. In an inner circle of divine fellowship, God is both an "I" and an "Us" (Isaiah 6:8). To each of the individual members of the Godhead, there are *the others.* The unifying factor that binds the three together as one is the selfless love that is the core essence of the Divine Being.

To believe in the biblical view of the Trinity is to see Deity as existing in dynamic relationship: God as both *self* and *other*, a singular personhood and a relational unity of three distinct persons.

To believe in a Trinity is to see Divinity living with a supreme will and desire to move in absolute self-giving motion toward the others.

To believe in a triune God is to believe that love is the foundational reality of this universe in which we find ourselves.

To *not* believe in a Trinity is to find one's self at a loss to understand what the Bible could possibly mean when it says, "God is love." Without the biblical truth of a tri-eternal Father-Son-Spirit Godhead, there is no logic capable of seeing God as existing in a state of love "before all things" were "made." God could only be seen as *self*, but not as *self* and *other* in love.

Now let's hear what Jesus had to say concerning what God was doing before Creation. Addressing the Father, the Savior prayed, "You [Father] loved Me before the foundation of the world" (John 17:24).

If Solomon's personified Wisdom is an Old Testament allusion to the pre-incarnate Christ, as Paul suggests (1 Corinthians 1:24), then the following words give us additional insight as to how the members of the Godhead interacted leading up to Creation:

"I [Christ] was beside Him [the Father] as a master craftsman; and I was daily His delight, rejoicing always before Him" (Proverbs 8:30).

"I was at His side each day, His darling and delight, playing in His presence continually" (NEB).

"Always enjoying His company" (TM).

Loving . . .

Delighting . . .

Rejoicing . . .

Playing . . .

Enjoying one another's company.

What an incredibly beautiful pre-Creation portrait of our God!

Do you see it?

Do you see what kind of person God really is?

For all of eternity past God has been engaged in the glorious reality of an other-centered love as ancient as Himself, living as a Trinity of intimate friendship.

What else can we say about God?

If not to expound His love, we can say very little, if anything, and actually know what we're talking about.

Can we speak intelligibly of His unborrowed, eternal existence, derived from no source more fundamental than Himself? To say that God has always been and that there was never a time when He was not, really amounts to saying nothing that we even remotely comprehend. It is a true statement, we believe, but not a productive line of study. All we can see in our world are points of origin, and to grasp the idea of a Matrix Life with no point of origin is simply out of our intellectual orbit. So we accept the biblical declaration, "from everlasting to everlasting, You are God," and then lay the topic down.

Can we speak of "the boundless immensity of God's universe"? To say it is *boundless* is to say it has no boundaries at all; it is endless. To say it is *immense* is to say it is limited to merely a space that is extremely large, but has an end. Which is it? We don't really know. That's why we speak of self-contradictory things like, "boundless immensity." We have a hunch that it is boundless, but what does that mean? We cannot even begin to imagine a point (a boundary) beyond which there is nothing else. What exactly would that boundary be? A wall? A chasm? What? And what would be the "nothing" beyond that boundary? Empty space? And yet empty space is far from nothing. It is indeed something. It is empty space. We can only conceive of more and more and more of something, because we cannot conceive of nothing. Here, again, as with God's existence, we simply do not know what we are talking about.

Shall we speak of His nature, as in the substance of which He is composed? Can we even use such words as *substance* and *composed* when talking about God? And yet, any words we come up with will most likely be synonyms of these, because all we know is substance and composition. Is He physical matter of some kind, like the flesh and bone and blood we're made of? After all, the Bible says God has "ears" that hear and "eyes" that see (Psalm 34:15), a "mouth" that speaks (Isaiah 1:20), a "face" that we will one day see (Revelation 22:4), and a "back" that Moses did see (Exodus 33:23). But is that His essential nature, or does He simply appear in material form in order to interact with us? Another Scripture says, "God is Spirit" (John 4:24). What is that? An invisible substance, or no substance at all? The Bible also says that the angels are "spirits" (Hebrews 1:14), and that each human being has a "spirit" (1 Corinthians 2:11, Ecclesiastes 12:7). So what is God made of? Well, for one thing, He's not made, so we cannot conceive of Him being made of anything. And yet He is, but we do not really know what He is in nature.

Can we say more about God's existence, about the dimensions of His universe, or about His nature? Certainly we can say more of the little we know. And when we have said all of the little we know, what have we really said? Approximately nothing at all. Nothing, that is, except the bare facts and vague hunches of things that elude our finite grasp.

So what can we really know and say about God? Is there no open door before us, no veil that may be penetrated? Is there any dimension of the Divine Being that we may plunge into with exploratory wonder? Can we learn and grow and soar in our knowledge of God in any fruitful line of contemplation?

Ah, yes, there is!

We may know the *character* of God! We may know that God is a real person, and what kind of person He is! We may ask the questions that really matter and receive answers.

What is God like at heart?

Does the question call you in?

How does He think and feel?

Does the prospect of such discovery excite you?

What makes Him move deep inside His Divine Being?

Does the possibility of moving in sync with Him arouse new urges within you?

What is the driving reason behind His deeds?

Do you find your heart reaching, feeling, moving toward Him, to know God on this level?

Nature, with its speechless disclosures, and biblical revelation, with its articulate descriptions, will eagerly answer to all such panting after God. There is a door flung wide open before our searching eyes and hungering hearts . . . into the character of God.

Peer far, not forgetting to look near!

Gaze high, not failing to search low!

Here is presented to our eager minds layer after layer, facet after facet, dimension after dimension of depth and texture and shape that we can comprehend, if we so desire. There stands before us an attractive form, just beyond the shimmering veil of Creation and the inspired Word.

Do you see it?

Squint and sweat if you must, but do not miss the fair image; for if you do, you will have missed all that truly matters. Engage your intellect and your emotions in riveted focus. Think and feel toward God with the best energies of your life . . . and the outcome is certain: with increasing acuity of sense and sensibility you will begin to see Him, feature after feature culminating to paint His true likeness on the inner canvas of your soul. You will come to know God as He is, and in that knowing you will find yourself falling in love, deeper and deeper as your vision sharpens. You will pass behind the veil into a growing awareness of the truth spoken by all of Creation and Revelation:

God is love . . .

God is love . . .

God is love . . .

you will hear the unmistakable whisper over and over again, until it is the only thing you know.

— Chapter Three —

Out of the Womb of Love

CREATION

Born to life, born to light,
    Born to love, but never night.
Born to risk, born to choose,
    Born to pain, but not to lose.

ONCE, GOD WAS all there was. At some time in eternal ages past, only the ineffable One existed as a triune fellowship of selfless, other-centered love. There was no conscious, freestanding life outside of the Father-Son-Spirit Trio. God alone constituted the complete whole of reality.

And yet, there was no lack. We can only imagine the picture to be utterly perfect, a ceaseless joy and peace flowing freely between them in their mutual love. But while there was no lack, there was desire—intense, burning desire—desire to create and love others, desire for the as-yet-uncreated you and me.

Perhaps we should not say God *needed* to create us, but we may definitely say He *wanted* to, which may place a higher value on us than necessity would permit. We may even venture to say that God's creation of us was inevitable, for God is love. Because God is love, God is Creator, for it is the nature of love to be centered on others outside of self. But there were no others. And yet, because God is infinite in power, it was within His ability to create others beside Himself, and hence others to love.

So He did.

How could He not do this wondrous thing that was in His power to do, this beautiful thing that was in His very nature to do? How could He not create others to love?

"Then God said, 'Let Us make man in Our image, according to Our likeness.' . . . So God created man in His own image; in the image of God He created him; male and female He created them" (Genesis 1:26-27).

God is an "Us." Therefore, His image was created as a "them," who could also be an "us." Makes sense. Reason it through with me.

To create is to make visible and/or audible the contents of one's heart and mind. A painting is first a picture in the artist's imagination or memory, then it is transferred to canvas. A song is first a conceptual sense coursing through the writer's emotional veins, then it is expressed in melody and lyric.

In principle, the same is true of God, only on an infinitely higher level. All of our human creative endeavors are merely dim shadows of the brilliant reality of God's power to create. When He ventured into the sublime work of making things outside Himself, He did so as an expression of Himself, as living reflections of His "image."

Within all of Creation, with the exception of the deformities and chaotic breakdowns imposed by sin, is discernable a single principle of life. Call it reciprocation, if you like. Call it *cause and effect*. Call it *the cycle of life*. Call it *the circle of beneficence*. But whatever you call it, the underlying meaning must be kept quite clear: all forms of life move in a circular motion, each individual piece receiving only to give. Every part is ultimately dependent for survival on its place in the giving-receiving design of the whole and destined for death if ever the connection is severed. Outward motion is the law of life. Stagnation is death. Everything is made to operate in dynamic give-and-receive relationship.

This is the meaning of all true law. Law is simply a word that refers to how things work when they operate as God designed them to, in harmony with His love, which is the blueprint of all Creation. While at first glance it appears as though there are a multitude of laws that govern life, it turns out, on closer observation, that all of these laws are simply various configurations of a single law. Everything in Creation is engineered so that each individual part is dependent upon receiving from other equally dependent parts, and in turn each part finds its health and meaning in giving to the others what has been received. There is a constant filling and emptying motion. It doesn't matter whether we're looking at ecology or economics, physiology or psychology, sociology or spirituality, business principles, agriculture, or even computer science—all functional systems are governed by relational dynamics. From the subatomic up to the cosmic level, all of Creation is simply layer after layer of a single principle repeatedly magnified and reconfigured to infinity. That principle is love, and God is its infinity.

Original Creation flowed from God's heart as a perfect mirror reflection of His character. Sin broke the mirror and scattered the fragments of glass among mutant perversions. And yet the Creator's likeness is still visible on every piece. Even with the fatal wounds of the fall upon its face, Creation still reflects the true image of its Maker. Any exceptions are the direct result of the disharmonizing influence of sin, which is self-centered at its core and therefore isolating in its effect. True science, working from the premise of a Benevolent Matrix, serves to rearrange the pieces so as to recognize the interlocking harmony of the whole and identify the variant mutations which are the work of an enemy.

God made and sustains the sun as the initiator of nature's circle of giving. As a symbol of Himself (Malachi 4:2), the sun is the source of a constant output of energy that is not fed by any other natural source more fundamental than itself. Radiant energy flows in a nonstop current from the sun. As the warm light bathes the soil, seeds germinate and spring to life. By an astounding process called *photosynthesis* the sun's energy is infused into the new plants. *Photo* means "light." *Synthesis* means "to compose or build." *Photosynthesis* means "to compose with light." (By the way, this is exactly how our characters are recreated in the plan of salvation. The new heart is composed by the light of the gospel.) As the light of the sun shines on a plant, the energy in the light is changed into a chemical structure of stored and organized energy, which fuels the building of additional tissue. In other words, the plant grows, resulting in leaves, flowers, fruit and seeds. Each seed is a living organism composed of actual stored energy from the light of the sun, prepared to germinate and bring forth plant life again and again in circular motion. The fruit is eaten by humans and animals, transferring the same light-energy to the various tissues of those living bodies. Through the process of digestion and assimilation, nutrients are transferred to the bloodstream and carried throughout the body to every vital organ. We then expend the received energy by living and growing, and, in turn, we cultivate and beautify the earth as benevolent stewards. The circle is complete.

Trace the circular path of H_2O. From the ocean, water evaporates upward to form clouds by means of the energy radiating from the sun. Rain then falls on the surface of the earth, absorbing and dissolving nitrogen and oxygen on its way down, forming nitric acids, which in turn saturate the soil as vital fertilizer. Rivers and streams are formed, which flow to lakes and seas, from which the very same water again evaporates upward to form clouds, to fall as rain yet again, and again, and again. The circle is a perpetual lesson in microcosm of the macro reality of God's love. Even on a molecular level water reveals relational interdependence as a triune composition. Two hydrogen atoms and one oxygen atom (H_2O) unify to form one water molecule. The three are one. Our entire ecosystem is an intricately designed ebb and flow of endless reciprocation—love illustrated.

Moving from ecology and physiology into psychology and sociology, the same circular pattern is evident. Excuse my simplification, but psychology basically boils down to mental health or mental illness resulting from perceived or real relational inequities with others and one's self, in some cases including hereditary or self-imposed chemical imbalance. Relationships in which there is a mutual exchange (a circle) of positive giving and receiving— respect, trust, integrity, kindness, sympathy and forgiveness—tend to yield mental and emotional confidence, self-respect, motivation, productivity and creativity, equating to positive mental health. Relationships in which one's focus becomes centered on self rather than others—deceit, manipulation, cruelty, hate, sexual perversion—produce a sense of isolation, insecurity, guilt, low self-worth, suspicion, phobia, and a lack of will to create, produce and even live. Hence, mental breakdown.

The reason mental health and mental illness are possible is because the human mind was designed in harmony with a single, immutable law—the law of love, having its origin in the mind of God. Our minds are like delicate, finely tuned machinery. We were engineered to only experience love, flowing out of us *to* others and flowing into us *from* others. Anything contrary to love deeply wounds our inner psyche. Disrespect, unkindness, lying, jealousy, hatred, sexual infidelity and the like hurt us. Why? Because to engage in such things is to transgress the integrity of our relationship with God and our fellow human beings by preferring self above others (1 John 3:4, Matthew 22:37-40). By sinning against God and others we literally violate our own inner being, tearing ourselves down on the mental and emotional level. Personified Wisdom declares, "He who sins against Me wrongs his own soul [psyche]; all those who hate Me love death" (Proverbs 8:36). By sinning we break the circle of love and thrust ourselves into a linear course of isolation, ultimately resulting in death.

Ezekiel described the appearance of God's universal order as "a wheel in the middle of a wheel" (Ezekiel 1:16). The Hebrew word here translated *wheel* means "to revolve," and communicates the idea of a circular motion. In light of this biblical concept, it is interesting to note that every branch of scientific study continues to discover one circle within another, within another, within another. Whether we look deeper and deeper to the infinitesimal, subatomic level, or higher and higher to the infinite, cosmic level, all we see is wheel within wheel within wheel. All we see is love.

Scripture is declaring literal truth, and not mere poetic hyperbole, when it says, "Since the creation of the world His invisible attributes are clearly seen, being understood by the things that are made, even His eternal power and Godhead" (Romans 1:20). Here Paul makes the astounding claim that the true character of God is clearly revealed in all He has made, "even," says the apostle, to the detailed degree of making known "His eternal power," which is love, and "Godhead," meaning the relational harmony of the Three who are One.

It is evident that the universe in which we live is essentially relational. It is a *universe* rather than a *multiverse* or a *monoverse*. Reality is fundamentally other-centered in its orientation. It is a complex construct of individual parts in constant outward-tending motion, pouring out of each *one* into the *others*. And yet, while all of Creation is patterned after the image of God, all things are not equal expressions of His glory. There are varying degrees of intricacy and detail from one level to the next. With this in mind, we now turn our attention to the crown of all Creation, the most complete revelation of the divine likeness: a man and a woman in love.

Humanity was created to be the highest manifestation of the love that is the core essence of God's character. By definition, love is essentially selfless and other-centered. As noted in the previous chapter, God is both "self" and "other." He can say on the one hand, "I AM," and on the other hand, "Let Us" (Exodus 3:14; Genesis 1:26-27). God is three ones and one three, which the Bible calls "the Godhead" (Romans 1:20); three individual persons who are one whole of selfless unity. Not $1 + 1 + 1 = 3$, but $1 \times 1 \times 1 = 1$. Love is the mysterious reality that defines God's plural yet singular personhood.

It follows, then, that a reproduction of God's "image" would of necessity be both *self* and *other,* each one choosing to make the *self* secondary to the *other.* Only thus could the likeness of God's love exist outside of the Trinity. Emerging from the womb of God's desire, there stood the man, Adam, an individual person conscious of himself and of his freedom. Contemplating the forthcoming finished product, God looked upon Adam and said, "It is not good that man should be alone; I will make him a helper comparable to him" (Genesis 2:18); or better translated, a counterpart or a second self. By strict biblical definition, Adam alone could not constitute a complete reproduction of God's image. There would need to be an*other* besides him*self.* Hence, the woman. There stood Eve, just as autonomous and free as her husband.

The Scripture reads in this pattern: "Our image = Our likeness = man[kind] = male and female = them" (Genesis 1:26-27). It is the reality of the *free self* in the mutually conscious presence of the equally *free other* that makes love possible. The man and the woman, each in love with the other above self, constitute the image of God. The women was taken out of the man as a distinct and separate self, just as the Father, Son and Spirit are distinct persons. Then she was again made one with the man in marriage, by voluntary love rendered in her freedom.

"Then the rib which the Lord God had taken from the man He made into a woman, and He brought her to the man. And Adam said: 'This is now bone of my bones and flesh of my flesh; she shall be called woman, because she was taken out of man!' Therefore a man shall leave his father and mother and be joined to his wife, and they shall become *one* flesh" (Genesis 2:22-24).

"Now Adam *knew* Eve his wife, and she conceived and bore Cain" (Genesis 4:1).

When the Bible says of Adam and Eve, they "became one flesh," and "knew" one another, and "she conceived," it is, of course, referring to the sealing of their love by sexual union. And yet their sexual oneness was the outermost layer of their love, symbolizing the deeper reality of two distinct persons giving the totality of self for the happiness of the other. The resulting pregnancy was the incarnation of their love, procreated in their own unified likeness. As the triune God is Creator by virtue of His love, so humanity was made to reproduce in their own image, and hence to show forth the truth of God's love. Thus was it always meant to be. As God's "offspring" (Acts 17: 28), brought forth from the womb of selfless love, it was His plan that all we would ever experience was the ceaseless joy of an endlessly deepening love relationship with Himself and with all the others born of our love.

And yet, there was an unavoidable risk.

— *Chapter Four* —

A Risk-Free
Relationship
MEANING

Are You a puppeteer,
     Pulling on my strings?
Is that all there is,
     To what life means?
Yet if you don't pull,
     I'm afraid I'll have to choose;
All blame and all excuses,
     Through freedom sure to lose.

IMAGINE THAT THE future of artificial intelligence has arrived. Robotics and computer technologies have developed to the point where spouses, children and friends are made to order in sophisticated manufacturing facilities.

You are a single woman, 30 years of age, with no prospect of marriage in sight. One evening an advertisement on TV catches your attention. The company is called "Perfect Person Companions." The ad is very impressive, complete with a 90-day, money-back guarantee. The best thing about the ad is that it promises a "Risk-Free Relationship," with absolutely no possibility that your "perfect person" will ever do anything other than what you want.

Although the idea seems a little weird, you are very lonely, and these computer companions are supposed to be so lifelike that none of your friends would ever know he (or rather, it) wasn't a real human. Of course, you would always know, but who cares, if he's perfect. So you call the 1-800 number given on the screen. In less than one week a catalog arrives in your mailbox. Page after page you browse through the possibilities. After much thought, you finally settle on Model DB-510, 170. The D in the model code stands for dark hair and skin. The B indicates blue eyes. A height of 5 feet, 10 inches is indicated by the number 510, and 170 specifies weight.

You place your order and wait. Allowing four to six weeks for delivery, the day finally arrives. As the delivery truck pulls into your driveway, you are nervous but excited. The truck driver unloads an unmarked coffin-size crate with a dolly and carefully places it on your living room floor.

A distracting thought crosses your mind, "Hey, that truck driver is cute."

"But I'm committed to someone else, so forget the truck driver," you think to yourself, pulling your mind back to your crated companion.

Then the trucker casually asks, "Would you mind if I came by sometime to say hi? Maybe we could have dinner together?"

"Ummm . . . well . . . " you stammer, "no, that wouldn't be possible . . . ummm . . . I'm married."

"Oh, I'm sorry, ma'am."

With that, he hurries away.

Turning your attention back to the large box on the floor, you wipe a little perspiration from your forehead.

"Here goes," you speak aloud to yourself and proceed to remove the lid with a pry bar.

"Wow!"

There he lay, more handsome than you had imagined, and so very real-looking. On his chest is an Instruction Manual, with the words on the cover:

"Warning—Do not turn on your new *Perfect Person Companion* without reading and following this manual first."

Page one explains that you must first insert into your personal home computer the disk provided. After answering a series of questions, the information is to be downloaded into your *Perfect Person Companion* by use of a special cable. The manual further explains, "The information you download will determine the personality, likes and dislikes and daily habits of your new *Perfect Person Companion*. But not to worry, if you don't get it all just right the first time, adjustments may be made to modify any disagreeable traits."

"This is better than I thought it would be," you muse to yourself. "I actually get to customize this guy to my own specifications."

Every woman's dream.

You consider throwing a party for yourself on the spot, but you get control of yourself and proceed. Eager for love, you quickly insert the disk and begin answering the questions as they appear on your screen.

1. What name would you like to give your *Perfect Person Companion?* (Cannot be changed.)

"Brock Branson Brightman," you type. It's always been your favorite name for a guy. After all, your name is Bethany Brenda Bebo and you like the idea of having the same initials.

2. What kinds of things would you like to hear first thing in the morning? Give at least four options. (Remember, the more information you download, the more realistic your *Perfect Person Companion* will be.)

You give it some thought and come up with a list of five different things you would love to hear in the morning.

    a. Good morning, Gorgeous!

    b. You look as lovely as you did yesterday.

    c. A long night's sleep detracts nothing from your beauty!

    d. I was dreaming about you all night, Sweetheart.

    e. I love your messy morning look.

3. How many times per month would you like breakfast served to you in bed?

You were hoping there would be a breakfast-in-bed feature.

■ a. Every day (You indulgent queen!)

☐ b. Vary between 5 to 10 times

☐ c. Other _____

4. Sense of humor type?

☐ a. Silly

☐ b. Sarcastic

■ c. Hilarious

☐ d. Charming

5. What is your favorite flower?

☐ a. Roses

☐ b. Carnations

■ c. Daisies

☐ d. Other _____

6. Public displays of affection?

■ a. Yes

☐ b. No

7. Personality type? (You may select one or a combo of two.)

■ a. Sanguine

☐ b. Phlegmatic

☐ c. Melancholy

☐ d. Choleric

8. IQ? (Best to choose a category equal to or just below your own.)
☐ a. Genius
☐ b. Intelligent
☐ c. Average
■ d. Moron

Once all the questions are answered, the downloading is slick and hassle-free. Following the Instruction Manual you plug in the special cord—one end into your computer, the other end into the nose of your husband-to-be. The nose-plug feature made it possible for the manufacturer to avoid having an unsightly, machine-looking plug somewhere on your companion's body.

"What an ingenious idea!" you think to yourself and giggle.

You are just seconds away from Brock's first consciousness, or whatever you want to call it. According to the Instruction Manual, in order to turn on your *Perfect Person Companion* all you have to do is give a single kiss anywhere on the face. The forehead would be easy, since the nose cord would have to be bent up to kiss his (its) lips. Besides, you don't really know him (it) yet, so a kiss on the lips would be inappropriate. Leaning down over his face, you wonder for a moment, "Is this really what I want?"

"Sure it is," you retort to yourself, "I want love, and Brock is gonna give it to me."

With that, you quickly kiss his (its) forehead.

Immediately, those beautiful blue eyes open, a smile comes to his (its) face, and he (it) stands up and speaks.

"Hi, I'm Brock Branson Brightman."

So began your romance with your custom-crafted *Perfect Person Companion.*

As for me, if I were a woman, I'd find it difficult to enjoy a sanguine moron with a hilarious sense of humor telling me upon waking that I'm beautiful while serving me breakfast in bed. But hey, we all have different tastes. That's what you wanted, and that's what you got. Of course, this was just part of the picture. There were over a hundred other questions to answer. By answering all of them you were able to create the man of your nightmares . . . I mean, dreams.

Granted, there were a few minor bugs to work out of the system. Minor, that is, compared to being single for life.

Bug Number One: The moron level IQ began to wear on you, so you upped it to the genius level, not realizing that the human intelligence quotient is a circle in which genius and moron are nearly the same. Actually, the fact that Brock was a moron was not that big of a deal. Lots of guys are. The big problem was that he (it) was a computerized robot, which made Brock seem more moronic than most moronic guys.

Bug Number Two: One morning Brock served you breakfast in bed while telling jokes so hilarious you laughed food out of your mouth. You changed the humor category from hilarious to silly. Why you thought a silly genius would be better than a hilarious moron, I don't know. In any case, it was becoming difficult to laugh at Brock's jokes, since they were your jokes preprogrammed into his (its) database.

Bug Number Three: When meeting new people, he (it) would get tongue-twisted with the three rapid-succession B's in Brock Branson Brightman. While the name could not be changed in the software, you were able to select an option that kept all introductions on a first-name basis. If anyone would ask for a middle or last name, there would be enough pause to eliminate the tongue-twisting malfunction.

Once the bugs were worked out, Brocky Baby turned out to be a really great guy. Everything was "perfect," just like the manufacturer promised. He was a consummate gentleman. Sensitive. Kind. Funny. Strong. And never sick. Whenever the old jokes or wit or romantic whispers got old, all you had to do was download some new ones in through his nose. In fact, there was a daily customization feature (DCF) that allowed you to customize any day in advance. If you wanted a really special date with Brock, it was a simple matter of downloading the information the day before. If you had a hair appointment, you could make sure Brock noticed with extreme excitement and big compliments. Or, if you knew you might have a bad day, it was an easy matter to make Brock want to spend the whole day alone in his crate.

What more could any woman ask for?

A lot, actually!

For the first two months, your "relationship" with Brock felt like heaven on earth. But then something began to dawn on you.

"Brock," you said one day, "something is missing from our relationship."

At first you couldn't put your finger on the problem. And then suddenly one day you realized the truth.

"Brock," you said with tears, "you don't love me anymore . . . or, actually, you never have."

"Of course I love you, Sweetheart, with all my heart," Brock replied just as you had programmed him.

"No you don't, because you don't have a heart."

"Of course I do, Sweetheart, with all my heart," Brock repeated, for lack of anything else to say, literally.

The words seemed reassuring, but somehow you couldn't believe him (it), as much as you wanted to.

"Woman, I think you're getting all worked up over nothing. I do love you," Brock stated firmly.

"Now that's weird," you wondered out loud, "I don't remember programming that into him (it)."

But you must have, because everything about Brock first comes from you. In fact, Brock is you. Whenever he (it) says anything kind, it's you talking to yourself. Whenever he (it) does anything sweet, it's you serving yourself. Brock doesn't love you. He (it) can't. He (it) is a mindless, heartless machine.

Realizing the truth, you looked at him (it) right in the eyes and said, "Brock, it's just not going to work out between us."

Brock looked deeply hurt. But how could he (it) be hurt?

Or happy?

Or sad?

Or mad?

Or anything at all?

Fortunately for you, all this became clear to your mind before the 90-day guarantee was up. Following the return instructions, you told Brock to get into his crate. He pled and cried (complete with tears) and gave some convincing arguments in favor of working out the relationship (preprogrammed into him by the manufacturer).

You almost softened, but resolved to hold your ground.

"Into your crate, Brock, now!"

And in he (it) went.

"Goodbye, Brock," you whispered with a sigh of relief, and closed the lid.

Calling the toll-free number, you made arrangements to have Brock returned. To your pleasant surprise, the same cute trucker who delivered Brock came to pick him up.

"Is that offer for dinner still on," you shyly asked with a smile.

"Ma'am," he replied, "I would never date a married woman."

Tripping over your tongue, you accidentally said, "I'm getting rid of my husband; he's in this box."

Needless to say, with a look of terror in his eyes, the cute truck driver fled, leaving the crated Brock behind. You had to schedule another pickup.

Yes, you were back to being single. But at least you now knew that the love of a robot is no love at all, no matter how "perfect."

— Chapter Five —

The Risk of Love
FREE WILL

To be all there was and yet make others
To stand beside You free;
Bespeaks Your selfless love so high,
Nay, shouts Your love to me.

Then You chased us through our night,
Our night of selfish hate;
You plunged forgetful of Yourself,
Into our guilty fate.

It's more than I can fully grasp,
This love, yes high, but low;
Yet to this quest I'll ever fly,
That knowing I might know.

R ISK: 1. POSSIBILITY OF loss or injury; peril. 2. a dangerous element or factor. 3. to expose to hazard or danger" (*Webster's*).

What do you think? Is "risk" a word that fits into your picture of God? Is it tolerable in your thinking that Almighty God could know anything like peril? Can you envision Him facing the real possibility of loss or injury? Would He be less than perfect, less than God, in your estimation, if anything in His very own creation threatened Him with actual danger? Does God's omnipotence make it impossible for anything to ever twist and turn out of His direct control? Was creation a risky venture for God, or was everything a foregone conclusion from His Divine vantage point? Can you conceive of a God of risk?

Or, wait a minute. Can you conceive of anything but a God who would put Himself at risk for others if need be? Can you see any other picture than a God who would fling Himself into harm's way, into the possibility of loss, for those He has made? Can you believe anything less of God than that He would genuinely love with utter self-abandon?

I can't!

A few moments contemplation reveals the breathtaking fact that God undertook a truly astounding venture by creating free moral agents. C.S. Lewis distills the profound reality now before us:

"In creating beings with free will, omnipotence from the outset submits to the possibility of . . . defeat. What you call defeat, I call a miracle: for to make things which are not *Itself* and thus to become. . . capable of being resisted by its own handiwork, is the most astonishing and unimaginable of all the feats we attribute to the Deity" (*The Problem of Pain*, pp. 129-130).

When God said to Adam and Eve, "Of every tree of the garden you may freely eat; but of the tree of the knowledge of good and evil you shall not eat" (Genesis 2:16-17), did He genuinely intend that they not eat of the forbidden tree? Was it really within their power to choose to eat or not to eat?

If so, we can only conclude with wonder that when God created free moral beings, He did indeed venture into the uncertain and potentially devastating realm of risk.

"But God is in control," you say, trying to salvage His stability.

He certainly is. But here's the vital point: God is in control in just the way He has chosen to be. He is under no obligation to be sovereign in the way we think He ought to be. The whole tenor of Scripture, indeed the very fact that God has any *living* enemies at all, informs us that He has chosen to exercise His sovereignty by granting real freedom, not shrinking back from the risk inherent in that freedom, rather than ruling with a dominating control.

The issue is not whether God *could* control every detail of our lives. Certainly He could, if it were in His heart to do so. But therein lies the point. It is not in His heart to do so. He rather has chosen to create us with the potential for love, which requires that we be endowed with actual freedom, which unavoidably allows for the risk that we might choose not to love Him in return. To exercise an absolute control would be safe, but void of any possibilities beyond self. Love is risky, but pregnant with potential for reproduction in its image.

Was it not within God's almighty power and infinite wisdom to create beings who could love Him and each other with absolutely no possibility of ever sinning?

No, it was not possible, even for Almighty God.

If such a statement is shocking to us, it is only because we have misunderstood the true nature of divine omnipotence. We like to define God's omnipotence, with little thought or explanation, by saying, "God can do absolutely anything; there is nothing impossible for Him."

There is no problem with this idea, as long as we mean exactly what we say: God can do any*thing*. To exaggerate the concept of omnipotence to include "non-things" is not helpful to God or to our picture of Him. Jesus taught us that "with God all *things* are possible"(Matthew 19:26). In response to this declaration, someone will inevitably ask questions like these:

"Can God make a square circle?"

"Can He make fire that is not hot, or water that is not wet, or two adjacent mountains with no valley between?"

Some Christians feel compelled to answer yes to such questions. "We can't understand it," they will say, "but since God is all-powerful, He can do anything. So He certainly could make a square circle, or anything else, and to believe otherwise would be a denial of His power. It's a mystery we must believe by faith, not by sight or reason."

Certainly there are mysteries, but this is not one of them. The only mystery here is why anyone would desire mystery where none is necessary. As C.S. Lewis has said, "Nonsense is still nonsense, even when we speak it about God." We may as well answer yes to the question, "Is God powerful enough to create something that both exists and does not exist at the same time?"

Actually, no, He can't, because the very nature of a created thing is existence. Any particular object or entity cannot both exist and not exist simultaneously. It either does or does not. Nor can God make fire that is not hot, for it is the nature of fire, by God's own design, to be hot. If we want to imagine fire that is not hot, or water that is not wet, or existing things that don't exist, or any other "non-thing," we have only succeeded in imagining silly notions of no actual substance. To say that God cannot do stupid stuff is not a denial of His omnipotence, but a higher reverence for it. The Bible says, on the one hand, "With God all things are possible." The Bible also says, "It is impossible for God to lie" (Hebrews 6:18). Is God less powerful in our eyes because He cannot lie? Of course not. Is He less powerful because He cannot make cold fire or a square circle? Certainly not. Is He lacking in power because He cannot create freewill beings for whom sin is impossible? Absolutely not, for the two ideas are mutually exclusive by very nature.

Perhaps the most significant "non-thing" God absolutely cannot do is save a person who chooses to be lost. This brings us to the real vital issue regarding God's sovereignty, namely the sovereignty of the free wills He has created adjacent to Himself. Scripture is clear that God desires all to be saved and none to perish (2 Peter 3:9). And yet the Bible is equally clear that the will of Almighty God shall not be fulfilled in this matter. Some free agents will, in fact, be eternally lost. God doesn't want them to be lost, but they will be. Even if God were to concentrate all His power on a single individual, He could not save that person without their freewill consent.

Sure, God could force the person to live forever in Heaven, but that wouldn't actually be salvation. It would be a confining, tormenting bondage. Salvation is not mere biological life forever sustained in the geographical location of Heaven. Salvation is complete psycho-emotional deliverance from sin—freedom from sin's lies about God, its guilt, its dominance, its physical effects and its death penalty. Stated from the positive angle, salvation is complete re-creation of God's selfless, other-centered love in our mental and emotional being. Salvation restores the truth about God's character of love in our understanding, restores to our hearts innocence and confidence before God, restores to our wills the motivational power to live in harmony with God's law of love, and finally restores perfect health and immortality to our bodies.

When salvation is understood to be deliverance from sin and restoration of God's love in the deep inner core of free moral agents, the vital role of free will becomes obvious. While behavior may be controlled by externally imposed force, love cannot be achieved by the same means. Only by love is love awakened, for love is the action of a free will to value and care for others above self.

Yes, God could have made a universe in which evil would be impossible, but that would be a universe in which love would be impossible as well. So He chose the risk of evil over the absence of love. If God had created "Perfect Person Companions," mere preprogrammed robots, such an act would have revealed a character entirely bent on self-serving. But the creation of freewill beings, persons distinct and autonomous from Himself, was an act of supreme and extreme selflessness and humility. Think about the implications. By creating free moral agents,

- God opened up His own future and the future of His universe to be shaped by the potentially capricious decisions of others beside Himself;
- God made Himself willingly accountable to others who could choose to love Him or not;
- God opened Himself up to the risk of infinite suffering and even infinite loss.

But what, exactly, does all this mean? How could the future of Almighty God be shaped by mere creatures of His own making? How could an omniscient God suffer and experience loss by the decisions of created beings? What, exactly, did God risk? It is a complex and staggering matter to consider, but here goes. This is what it looks like to me.

God knew that if He created freestanding others outside of Himself, He would love them above Himself. To love them less than Himself would, of course, pose no risk at all. If they stepped out of line, it would be a simple matter to obliterate them without a second thought. But that could not be the case with God, for "God is love," and that love is a reality of absolute other-centeredness. Once they were in existence, each one would be as real and distinct as God Himself in individual personhood. The value of each one would be literally infinite, since God is infinite and He would love each one above Himself. To lose even one of them, any one of them, would constitute an infinite loss, and would strike God's heart with infinite pain. It would be impossible to let them go without extending the Divine Self into the realm of infinite self-sacrifice to save them. To create persons who could enter into the experiential ecstasy of His love, He would need to make them free, and therefore capable of rejecting His love. And He would need to be prepared to give His own life and risk the possibility of eternal loss.

The Fall was not a divinely ordained inevitability, but merely a human possibility that God hoped never to face. Adam and Eve were given a real choice in the matter. They did not have to choose sin over love. The Fall was unnecessary. But against all divine desire, fall they did. And so began the deep aching in God's heart, and with it a stormy torrent of complex and rational emotions that had been forever enfolded in the soft inner core of His love. (Oh, that He whom we now love had never felt such torn and broken feelings on our account!) The sacrifice must now be made, attended with a risk that made the unfallen universe shutter with horror and the demonic host quiver with diabolical determination to make their blows count.

When Christ became a human being, was it a divine charade intended to give the appearance of risk and sacrifice, or was it a real condescension with the real possibility of failure? Could Christ have sinned? Or was it an impossibility, therefore rendering His struggle with temptation a hoax He hoped we would believe? Was the struggling, tempted, agonizing, bleeding, dying life of Christ a divine lie, or was it the truth of His experience?

Fallen human nature was uncharted territory for God prior to the incarnation of Christ. With infinite intelligence and wisdom He could look into our experience with sin and comprehend it, but not until He entered into our humanity did He know our situation *experientially*. Of God non-incarnate, James said, "God cannot be tempted" (James 1:13). Of God incarnate, Paul said, "He was in all points tempted as we are" (Hebrews 4:15). These Scriptures either express two truly distinct dimensions of divine experience, or we would have to conclude that they speak falsehood.

While the triune God pursued the plan for our salvation fully intending to succeed, and fully confident that their love would prevail, it is an unavoidable fact that the sacrifice of self involved in that plan would have to be genuine and not staged. Jesus really did become a member of the human race, forever to retain that nature as His own. He really did undergo severe temptation with the actual possibility of failure and eternal loss. He really did enter the dark psychological realm of our sin and guilt with the torturous sense of eternal separation from the Father. His character really was tested to the utmost to see if God does truly love others, even His enemies, above Himself. God staked the stability of the universe on the raw energy of His love apart from any other power. Under no circumstance would He resort to force or manipulation to hold Himself up. Love alone would prove itself of sufficient strength to conquer sin, or not.

If Christ had sinned, what would the outcome have been? What would have been the result if one of the members of the Godhead had become a sinner?

For starters, the salvation of the human race would have been forfeited. We all would have been lost, and God would have suffered that loss.

Secondly, if we take Scripture to mean what it says—"Sin, when it is full-grown, brings forth death" (James 1:15)—the fall of Christ would have entailed, not only the loss of the human race, but also the loss of His own eternal life. Exactly what that would have meant to the Father and the Holy Spirit, we have no way to fully or perhaps even slightly comprehend. The very thought is nightmarish while we ponder it fully awake.

Beyond the loss of Christ, the whole universe of created intelligences, angels and populated worlds throughout the cosmos would have been thrown into confusion, chaos and war. Every question and accusation raised by Satan in his war against God would have tormented the minds of all rational beings. The unity of God's kingdom would have been broken up into conflicting factions. The universe at large would have become like our war-torn world of fallen men and demons.

Three fascinating quotations comprehend something of this picture:

"Remember that *Christ risked all;* 'tempted like we are,' He staked even *His own eternal existence* upon the issue of the conflict. *Heaven itself was imperiled* for our redemption. At the foot of the cross, remembering that for one sinner Jesus would have yielded up His life, we may estimate the value of a soul" (*General Conference Bulletin*, December 1, 1895).

"Satan in Heaven had hated Christ for His position in the courts of God. ... He hated Him who pledged Himself to redeem a race of sinners. Yet into the world where Satan claimed dominion God permitted His Son to come, a helpless babe, subject to the weakness of humanity. He permitted Him to meet life's peril in common with every human soul, to fight the battle as every child of humanity must fight it, *at the risk of failure and eternal loss.*

"The heart of the human father yearns over his son. He looks into the face of his little child, and trembles at the thought of life's peril. He longs to shield his dear one from Satan's power, to hold him back from temptation and conflict. To meet a bitterer conflict and a more *fearful risk*, God gave His only-begotten Son, that the path of life might be made sure for our little ones. 'Herein is love.' Wonder, O heavens! And be astonished, O earth!" (*The Desire of Ages*, p. 49).

"Many claim that it was impossible for Christ to be overcome by temptation. Then He could not have been placed in Adam's position; He could not have gained the victory that Adam failed to gain. If we have in any sense a more trying conflict than had Christ, then He would not be able to succor us. But our Savior took humanity, with all its liabilities. He took the nature of man, with the possibility of yielding to temptation" (*The Desire of Ages*, p. 117).

In this chapter I have attempted to explain a dimension of God's love far too high for human comprehension, at least for mine. Please do overlook my frail effort where you see I have not done the subject justice, and appreciate the central idea for its own value. It is truly unfathomable that the self-existent, eternal God would love people like you and me, mere created beings and sinners besides, more than His own life. Even a dim realization of this truth makes me want to flee away in humility, and at the same time run into His embrace with adoring love and worship. I pray it will impact your heart in the same way.

— *Chapter Six* —

An Unlikely Backdrop for Betrayal

DIVINE INTENT

Crack the riddle of evil's reason,

    Find an answer to Satan's treason;

If you can, you've made excuse,

    For sin's a mystery we can't deduce.

W HILE THERE WAS risk involved in the creation of beings with free will, there was no just or rational cause for sin to ever emerge. Reading the Genesis account of Creation gives us the distinct impression that God was aiming to establish an atmosphere in which love would forever flourish as the only motivational force. In the story there are a number of elements, ever so obvious, that communicate the Creator's desire for an intimate friendship with Adam and Eve. We can't help but notice behaviors on God's part that were clearly oriented toward love:

- beautiful surroundings
- extravagant gift-giving
- special time together
- protective arrangements

Beautiful Surroundings

So much of God's friendly personality and benevolent character come through in the biblical record of Creation. As the account unfolds, we see Him moving about, shaping and arranging the pieces of an emerging work of art. He is obviously excited about pleasing someone.

"God created . . . God moved upon . . . God called . . . God made . . . God . . . divided . . . God . . . gathered together . . . God formed . . . God breathed" (Genesis 1-2).

Divine love is here demonstrated as the outflowing of creative energy in the making of beautiful things for others to enjoy.

There is "light," composed of a full spectrum of color.

There is "water," shimmering in the light, swelling, descending, flowing, reflecting.

There is the "firmament," the visible arc of the sky mirroring the rich, blended color of "the earth" and "the sea."

The sky is studded with "two great lights" and a multitude of "stars."

"The waters abound with an abundance of living creatures" of every shape and color imaginable.

"Birds fly above the earth across the face of the firmament of the heavens," simply to be seen and heard for the sheer pleasure they give.

"Living creatures" walk and hop and roll and run over land covered with lush vegetation. Some are of solemn appearance to arouse deep contemplation. Some are ever so funny to prompt laughter. Some are majestic beyond description to awaken a sense of utter amazement.

As the living, fluid masterpiece takes on form and feature, the One who is Artist, because He is Lover, speaks words of satisfaction at the creative expressions flowing from His eager heart:

"God saw that it was good . . . good . . . good . . . good . . . good . . . very good" (Genesis 1-2).

Meaning what, exactly?

Certainly it is functional as a system. But mere functionality is not what the Creator has in mind, though functionality is vital to His purpose. He is more than an engineer; He is an artist with a lover's heart. It is fascinating, then, but not surprising, that the Hebrew word *tob*, here simply translated "good," has a much richer meaning: "Beautiful, bountiful, cheerful, fair, fine, joyful, kindly, loving, pleasant, wealth" (*Strong's Concordance*). The Creation is "good" in the sense that it is extremely rich with capacity to impart pleasure.

And why is it all made so incredibly beautiful? Why such extravagance and attention to detail? Why is it put together with such high potential for pleasure?

Why else?

Because it is all a gift of love!

Extravagant Gift-Giving

True to His heart, true to His selfless identity, God created the earth and all its wonders as a gift for others. He is the One,

"Who created the heavens,

Who is God,

Who formed the earth and made it,

Who has established it,

Who did not create it in vain,

Who formed it to be inhabited" (Isaiah 45:18).

The Genesis record shows God, the Artistic Lover, creating living beings as recipients of all He has made. They are unique among the vast scope of created things, in that they are conscious persons who are capable of noticing their surroundings and experiencing the pleasures those surroundings afford. They are the final act of Creation, and all that was made before them was crafted with them in mind.

"The Lord has been mindful of us . . . Who made heaven and earth. The heaven, even the heavens, are the Lord's; but the earth He has given [as a gift of love] to the children of men" (Psalm 115:12, 15-16).

Imagine Adam and Eve awaking to their first few moments of life. How delighted they must have been to open their eyes and look into the intensely passionate eyes of their Maker. Everything that greeted their newly formed senses excited cheer and pleasure. Having given them the gift of life itself, God immediately proceeded to lavish additional gifts upon them.

First, "God blessed them" (Genesis 1:28).

The gift of blessing!

I love this word. It means that God made them happy by affirming and adoring them. I can imagine the blessing something like this:

"Welcome to life in this world I have made for you. I am Elohim, your Creator. I have cherished the thought of you for a very long time. Now, finally, your time has come. You are alive. So perfect, so very good and beautiful. Look around you. Listen to the lovely sounds. All of this is for you, from Me. I love you."

He gave them the gift of dominion, which means they were free to cultivate and be creative: "Be fruitful and multiply; fill the earth and subdue it; have dominion over . . . every living thing" (Genesis 1:28).

He gave them the gift of tasty, nourishing food to eat: "God said, 'See, I have given you every herb that yields seed which is on the face of all the earth, and every tree whose fruit yields seed; to you it shall be for food'" (Genesis 1:29). "And out of the ground the Lord God made every tree to grow that is pleasant to the sight and good for food. The tree of life was also in the midst of the garden" (Genesis 2:9).

He gave them one another, the gift of companionship, sexuality and the remarkable ability to procreate in their own blended image: God "made . . .

a woman, and He brought her to the man" (Genesis 2:22). "Male and female created He them . . . and God said to them 'Be fruitful and multiply'" (Genesis 1:27-28). "They shall become one flesh" (Genesis 2:24).

He gave them a special garden home that He Himself had planted: "The Lord God planted a garden eastward in Eden, and there He put the man [and the woman] whom He had formed" (Genesis 2:8). While the earth as a whole was somewhat a wilderness that they were to have the privilege of subduing into beautiful order, there was one spot that was perfected for them by God's own hands. *Eden* means "pleasure," a name signifying God's intention for the couple. Adam and Eve lived an experience of extreme pleasure by the Creator's design. All of their senses—sight, hearing, touch, taste, and smell—were continually flooded with holy, pleasure-inducing stimuli.

Special Time Together

Those who love one another are eager to engage their hearts and minds in fellowship. No relationship can be expected to deepen without the individuals spending consistent, quality time together. Genesis suggests that God probably spent personal time with Adam and Eve once each day for an unspecified period of time, and once each week for the entire day:

"They heard the sound of the Lord God walking in the garden in the cool of the day" (Genesis 3:8).

"God blessed the seventh day and sanctified it [set it apart for special use], because in it He rested from all His work which God had created and made" (Genesis 2:3).

"The Sabbath was made for man" (Mark 2:27).

The Sabbath was set aside, according to Isaiah, as a special time in which human beings would find "delight . . . in the Lord" (Isaiah 58:14).

Can you imagine the kind of interaction that must have occurred between the unfallen couple and their Creator? Certainly those were times of mutual delight in one another's friendship. No doubt Adam and Eve had endless questions about God, His vast universe, the other worlds, the mysteries of nature and themselves. And no doubt God gave them incredibly engaging answers, as their infinitely wise Teacher and the Maker of all things. Day after day, week after week, the divine-human friendship deepened with every new engagement.

Protective Arrangements

The placement of "the tree of the knowledge of good and evil" in Eden is a source of confusion to many people. Some see it as a set-up, as if God wanted humanity to fall. Others see it as an unnecessary test. "If the tree hadn't been there in the first place," they reason, "there would have been no restriction to violate and therefore no possibility of sin."

In truth, if there had been no such arrangement, there would have been no choice and therefore no possibility of real love. The tree did not represent narrow restriction, but rather enormous freedom. It wasn't a trap, but rather an unavoidable truth. Where love is the goal, freedom is the only way to get there. By definition, love means voluntary devotion to others above self. Force, coercion and manipulation are ways of relating that are diametrically opposed to the existence of love. In order for love to be possible, it must also be possible not to love. Because God made human beings for a love relationship with Himself, He made them truly free.

A more careful look at the record in Genesis reveals that the tree of the knowledge of good and evil was a protective arrangement intended to preserve love. It represented a restriction placed on Satan, limiting his access to Adam and Eve, while granting them the freedom essential for love to exist. The fact that God warned them about this one particular tree suggests that the enemy could only approach them at that single location if they chose to go there. Satan could not pursue them. The possibility of sin entering our world was made as remote as possible, while preserving the integrity of genuine freedom.

Here is the picture before us:

Beautiful Surroundings, to enliven the senses and calibrate the heart to the expectation of good things.

Extravagant Gift-Giving, to express God's deepest devotion and His desire for friendship.

Special Time, for focused attention, affection and affirmation, to enjoy the pleasure of one another's company.

Protective Arrangements, to jealously guard the relationship and preserve its free integrity.

All who are lovers at heart read the Genesis account of Creation and nod their heads with a smile. They know the behavior pattern of love. God so obviously followed that pattern. Indeed, He originated the pattern for all true lovers to follow. He created the perfect environment for friendship to forever flourish.

So what went wrong? This was no logical backdrop for betrayal. We see no flaw in God's relationship to Adam and Eve. No selfishness on His part to awaken selfishness in them. No cruelty toward them. No enslaving dominance over them. Indeed, not even a single lack existed to create a vacuum of need or a reason for treachery. Sin was a completely irrational response to this incredible love. There is only one conceivable way betrayal could occur against such a God as this, in such a setting as this.

Deception!

They must have been led to see God in a false light.

—Chapter Seven—

The Fall(ing Out
of Love)
SIN

Seductive arts, plied to steal,
Genius mind bent to kill;
In your embrace my heart feels cold,
'Neath your spell my core grows old.

I've loved another, sweet to taste,
I'm lured afar, true love's the place.
I'm not yours, so let me go,
My answer, firm, to you is No!

THE FALL OF mankind was less like the rebellion of a servant and more
like the adultery of a lover, less like the anarchy of a kingdom subject and
more like the betrayal of a friendship. No play on words intended, the Fall of
man was a *falling out of love* with God. Conversely, salvation is a falling back
in love with Him whom we have spurned with our unfaithfulness.

The most emotionally charged portrayals of God's heart in Scripture are
those in which He likens Himself to a faithful husband whose wife is engaged
in an illicit affair with another lover:

"'When you were born, no one cut your umbilical cord or washed you or
rubbed you with salt or wrapped you in cloths. No one took enough pity on
you to do any of these things for you. When you were born, no one loved
you. You were thrown out in an open field. Then I passed by and saw you
squirming in your own blood. You were covered with blood, but I wouldn't
let you die. I made you grow like a healthy plant. You grew strong and tall
and became a young woman. Your breasts were well-formed, and your hair
had grown, but you were naked. As I passed by again, I saw that *the time
had come for you to fall in love.* I covered your naked body with my coat and
promised to love you. Yes, I made a marriage covenant with you, and you
became Mine.' This is what the Sovereign Lord says.

"'Then I took water and washed the blood off you. I rubbed olive oil
on your skin. I dressed you in embroidered gowns and gave you shoes of the
best leather, a linen headband, and a silk cloak. I put jewels on you—bracelets
and necklaces. I gave you a nose ring and earrings and a beautiful crown to
wear. You had ornaments of gold and silver, and you always wore clothes
of embroidered linen and silk. You ate bread made from the best flour, and
had honey and olive oil to eat. Your beauty was dazzling, and you became a
queen. You became famous in every nation for your perfect beauty, because I
was the one who made you so lovely.' This is what the Sovereign Lord says.

"'But you took advantage of your beauty and fame to sleep with everyone who came along. You used some of your clothes to decorate your places of worship, and just like a prostitute, you gave yourself to everyone'" (Ezekiel 16:4-16, TEV).

There are those reading these words who know firsthand the deep anguish of having your love rejected. How intensely painful are the feelings of a jilted lover! What is it like to love someone with all the energy of your very life, only to have that person despise you in return? Undoubtedly, there is no greater pain that ever courses through the emotional veins of a human being. This is precisely why God chose to paint on our minds the heartbreaking image of adultery to represent the terrible reality of sin. Once that picture is sketched before us, He says, in essence, "This is how I see your sin, and how I feel it." From God's standpoint, our sin feels like the betrayal of His love, not like the breaking of impersonal rules.

And yet, as horrific as the image of adultery is, it falls far short of communicating how truly agonizing our sin is for God. We all know, whether we've stopped to think about it or not, that the measure of one's emotional pain is directly proportional to one's measure of love. As I pointed out in a previous book, *See With New Eyes*, the more deeply we love, the more intensely we hurt when our love is spurned. If God's love is infinitely greater than ours, and it is, then His pain at our infidelity is infinite in its intensity, far exceeding the pain we experience when our love is cast aside.

When we remember and truly believe that God brought us into existence to be His intimate friends, not mechanical robots or mindless slaves, sin appears to be the low and ugly thing it really is. Sin is not simply a matter of breaking lifeless rules written on paper or engraved in stone. Sin is the breaking of God's heart, a piercing of His living, pulsating love. It is a violation of His selfless devotion, taunting in His tear-streaked face, "You live for me, but I'm going to live for myself. I don't love You. So get out of my life."

A single line from a familiar book epitomizes the original fall of man and every sin to follow: "Selfishness took the place of love" (*Steps to Christ*, p. 17). What the Bible calls sin this more modern author identifies as the anti-love force of self-centeredness. This way of defining sin is clearly the intent of Scripture and is easily constructed with just a few verses. Put the pieces together with me.

1. The most straightforward biblical definition of sin is found in 1 John 3:4 (KJV): "Sin is transgression of the law."

2. The most straightforward biblical definition of the law is found in Romans 13:10: "Love is the fulfillment of the law."

3. The most straightforward biblical definition of love is found in three key verses: "Greater love has no one than this, than to lay down one's life for his friends" (John 15:13).

"The love of Christ compels us . . . that those who live should live no longer for themselves" (2 Corinthians 5:14-15).

"Love . . . does not seek its own" (1 Corinthians 13:4-5).

If sin is transgression of God's law, and God's law is love, and love is to live for others above self, then it is clear that sin is self-centeredness, which violates God's law of other-centered love. All thoughts and words and actions that are oriented toward self-serving at the expense of others are sin.

There are basically only two things happening in the universe: love and sin, other-centeredness and self-centeredness. This is no oversimplification. It is the absolute, inescapable truth. Love is the permanent, changeless law of life for the universe. It's not going anywhere, not running out, not diminishing or passing away. For all eternal ages past, love was the solitary, pervasive reality of the immortal life of God Himself.

Sin, on the other hand, is an aberration, a perversion, a transitory intruder sucking in one breath of stolen air, rearing its ugly head in the midst of God's natural order, and then passing away into eternal night. Because sin is essentially anti-love, it is, by extension, an anti-creational force as well. It is a chaos-producing, entropy-prompting, death-dealing power, winding down to an infinite nil, a lifeless nothing, to be as though it had not been, because, in fact, its life was never viable. Sin cannot sustain itself or its victims, because sin divides all its participants into one individualistic *I* after another, demanding that each one live only for *the self* with no primary regard for *the others*. The eventual net outcome is isolation of the self from all others by means of selfish deeds—greed, dishonesty, hate, manipulation, jealousy, lust, murder and the like. Self-centeredness is the common denominator of all sin, for sin takes and consumes without giving in return. Its very nature is to violate the only life-giving, life-sustaining law there is, God's law of love. Therefore, sin pursues death as its final end. "Sin, when it is full-grown, brings forth death" (James 1:15).

Satan achieved the fall of man by means of a lethal deception about God, geared toward stealing God's love from the human heart and arousing self-centeredness in its place. The lie was formulated with a specific intent to deny the existence of love in God's character. Notice the serpent's seductive reasoning:

"Now the serpent was more cunning than any beast of the field which the Lord God had made. And he said to the woman, 'Has God indeed said, 'You shall not eat of every tree of the garden'? And the woman said to the serpent, 'We may eat the fruit of the trees of the garden; but of the fruit of the tree which is in the midst of the garden, God has said, 'You shall not eat it, nor shall you touch it, lest you die.' Then the serpent said to the woman, 'You will not surely die. For God knows that in the day you eat of it your eyes will be opened, and you will be like God, knowing good and evil'" (Genesis 3:1-5).

According to this account, Satan approached the infant human race with "cunning," meaning an intent to deceive. It is clear that God is the target under siege; His character is the subject of the deception. The lie has three obvious components:

1. *God is restrictive.* The Creator had opened before Adam and Eve a vast horizon of liberty and had specified a minor protective restriction: "Of every tree of the garden you may freely eat; but of the tree of the knowledge of good and evil you shall not eat" (Genesis 2:16-17).

Satan put a negative spin on God's arrangement, stating it in terms of extreme restriction and zero liberty: "Has God indeed said, 'You shall not eat of every tree of the garden'?" (Genesis 3:1).

2. *God is a liar.* This picture of God was communicated in the words, "You will not surely die," a direct denial of God's truthfulness. The implication was that God lied in order to keep them confined under His restrictive bondage.

3. *God is self-centered.* "For God knows that in the day you eat of it your eyes will be opened, and you will be like God, knowing good and evil" (Genesis 3:5). Here the subtle message was that God was keeping from them something that would be for their higher good.

The subtle message woven throughout the Deceiver's words is that only self-centeredness would prompt God to keep from them the greater liberty of equality with Himself. By accepting the lie that God did not truly love them above Himself, Adam and Eve short-circuited the human heart's ability to engage in love; for we are utterly dependent on believing and receiving

His love in order to give love from our own lives. Love is derived from God as its only source. If we do not see it in Him, we cannot manufacture it in ourselves. Once Adam and Eve chose to come under the liar's spell, untainted love became a psychological, emotional and behavioral impossibility for the human race, apart from radical divine intervention.

The Genesis account describes the immediate effect of sin in these words:

"Then the eyes of both of them were opened, and they knew that they were naked; and they sewed fig leaves together and made themselves coverings" (Genesis 3:7). Before their fall, "they were both naked, the man and his wife, and were not ashamed" (Genesis 2:25).

What was happening here? What was the nature of this change?

Simply this: before sin entered the picture, Adam and Eve were completely other-centered in their consciousness, focused on God and one another. They were living in complete harmony with God's law of love. What they did see in themselves was the power and privilege to love and serve others. Hence there was no shame in their self-awareness, no sense of guilt in their nakedness of body or soul. But sin radically altered all this by shifting their focus from others to self. When they became self-serving, they became self-conscious and distinctly ashamed of what they saw in themselves.

Covering themselves with fig leaves was a vain attempt to hide from themselves and from God in order to evade the truth of their guilt. They felt this need because of the deception about God's character that lay at the foundation of their fall. Under the intoxicating influence of an arbitrary, self-serving picture of their Creator, they could no longer conceive of Him as the loving Father and Friend they once knew. The idea that He would respond to their sin with mercy did not occur to them. Therefore they expected rejection upon their next encounter with Him. Once Satan led them into sin, he then applied leverage to his deception by taking up the role of accuser (Revelation 12:9-10), with whispers of condemnation intended to impersonate the voice of God. In the dark shadows of Satan's lie regarding God's character, the Deceiver suggested that God would not forgive their sin. They imagined that the shame they felt toward themselves was from God, whom they now saw as a restrictive, selfish enemy. They "hid themselves from the presence of the Lord" because they were now "afraid" of Him (Genesis 3:8-10).

By asking the question, "Who told you that you were naked?" (verse 11), God disassociated Himself from their shame, suggesting that He was not its source. In the next question—"Have you eaten from the tree of which I commanded you that you should not eat?"—God pointed to their sin itself as the true source of their shame. In other words, the guilt they felt was the real and appropriate response of conscience to their wrong doing. God was not imposing condemnation upon them as an arbitrary punishment for an act that was otherwise innocent and harmless. There was actual guilt and harm in their sin. They were, in fact, wrong. They did, in fact, violate the very law of all Creation. In so doing they chose to pursue a course contrary to the law of their own nature, which God designed in harmony with His law of love.

In the New Testament, Jesus identified Satan's character as a twisted composition of three evils: deception, theft and murder. By lying, he steals; by stealing, he kills.

"He was a murderer from the beginning, and does not stand in the truth, because there is no truth in him. When he speaks a lie, he speaks from his own resources, for he is a liar and the father of it" (John 8:44).

"The thief does not come except to steal, and to kill, and to destroy" (John 10:10).

By means of deception, Satan has stolen the human heart from God, and has stolen a clear sense of God's love from the human heart. To destroy us by that theft is his ultimate purpose. With evil genius he crafts all his lies to contribute to the one lie first forged of jealousy in his dark heart: *God does not love you, but lives only for Himself. Therefore flee from His dominating control and live only for yourself.*

As "the god of this world," the Great Deceiver has "blinded the minds of them which believe not, lest the light of the glorious gospel of Christ, who is the image of God, should shine unto them" (2 Corinthians 4:4, KJV).

Did you catch the full significance of what Paul is telling us here? Perhaps more clearly than any other passage of Scripture, this single verse informs us of Satan's strategy to work our eternal ruin. The focus of his attack is our "minds." More specifically, his plan for our minds is "blindness." This indicates that the warfare centers on the matter of perception. There is something Satan does not want us to see clearly. It is his studied aim to block from our vision "the image of God." His single-minded goal is to keep God's true character of love hidden from our understanding.

After exposing the enemy's scheme, Paul then proclaims God's answer to the lie leveled against Him:

"The same God who said, 'Out of darkness let light shine,' has caused His light to shine within us, to give the light of revelation—the revelation of the glory of God in the face of Jesus Christ" (2 Corinthians 4:6, NEB).

Our blindness of mind is healed as we look to Jesus, believing that in Him we see "the best picture of God we'll ever get" (2 Corinthians 4:6, TM). The spell of darkness cast upon our first parents is broken when we allow the revelation of God's glorious love in Jesus to shine into our hearts.

Then God's most heartfelt anticipation will be realized:

"As I passed by again, I saw that the time had come for you to fall in love. I covered your naked body with my coat and promised to love you. Yes, I made a marriage covenant with you, and you became Mine" (Ezekiel 16:8, TEV).

Fallen humanity is redeemed as we fall back in love with God.

— *Chapter Eight* —

Liar's Motive
SATAN

The lie is deceptive . . .
     Can you name it?
The lie is disguised . . .
     Do you even know if you believe it?
The lie is dark . . .
     Have your eyes adjusted?
The lie is dangerous . . .
     You'll think you can see!
The lie disfigures . . .
     Are you really who you want to be?
And the lie is a mask worn by the thief,
     Who steals by the changes wrought by his lie.

Stolen is sight . . .
     The third eye is blind.
Stolen is trust . . .
     The Friend now appears foe.

Stolen is reason . . .

    The foe that is Friend appears arbitrary.

Stolen is innocence . . .

    Eyes shift in the dark while the heart trembles.

Stolen is love . . .

    "There is none but I, and I alone!"

Stolen is the will . . .

    He who will not love eventually cannot.

And the thief is a murderer, when all is told and taken,

    Who lied to steal and stole to kill.

The killing is subtle . . .

    It feels like life with the sensations it gives.

The killing is slow . . .

    Do you perceive it happening?

The killing is homicide that can only occur as suicide . . .

    Why do we invite the murderer in?

The killing is vindictive . . .

    To hurt the Life-giver is the motive.

—Chapter Nine—

Concealed To Reveal

JUSTIFICATION

He took me in His human arms,
Calming all my fears;
He loved me with His human heart,
I tasted of His tears.
Resting there upon His chest,
Feeling peace, no dread,
He whispered words I could now bear,
"I'm God, the One you've fled."

Long ago, in a not so faraway place called Emeth, there lived a king of undisputed reign. His name was Mashal Melek Attiq, meaning "King of Ancient Power" in the artistic language of that land. His empire was vast. Just how vast, no one really knew. But one thing was clear to all: there was no king greater than he, and no kingdom as powerful as his.

An air of wonder, even perplexity, surrounded the dominion of Mashal. For, as you have probably heard, he built his empire without war, contradicting the history of all other kingdoms ever to exist. Every territory under his rule had been won, not conquered, village after village, city after city, by the spreading fame of his kind and just ways of governing. All who were his subjects wanted to be. Almost all. There was an exception.

Kazab.

One battle had occurred, just one, at the beginning of Mashal's reign, with the much-feared warrior king, Kazab, of renowned power and infamous cruelty. Kazab was known to be so fierce in war, and Mashal had conquered him so quickly and without loss or injury, that all were persuaded of Mashal's incomparable power. The good king didn't seem to care much for hearing or telling the story himself. Even in his conquest over Kazab, he did not kill his enemy, but placed him in exile.

Surrounding this single war, a rumor was whispered about concerning the king that, for its intrigue alone, would not die away. The story had been crafted into a terrible narrative and was told by firelight whenever anyone dared to question if Mashal was truly as strong as most people believed. His gentleness might be seen as weakness in the dim eyes of the foolish, but this dark tale would quickly strike terror into their hearts.

It was thought that the rumor originated from the lips of Kazab, and on that ground was regarded as false by most. There were some, however, who cared not where it originated—it just sounded like the sort of thing that would be true. So they believed it, while yet hoping it was not true, if only for their own sakes.

The rumor was that Mashal had a dark side that no one would ever want to awaken. His gentleness, it was said, was an act to hide a truly ruthless heart. All one need do to see the mask fall and receive his cruel wrath was to defy his will in the least particular.

Due partly to the dark rumor, and partly to the fact of his immense power and wealth, Mashal was faced with one serious problem that brought him pain untold, day and night.

The king was in love.

Some of his wisest counselors could not understand his perplexity.

"How could this be a problem?" they reasoned. "You are the Sovereign Monarch. Surely any woman would say yes to your overtures. How dare any do otherwise!"

But that was precisely the point. Herein was the king's dilemma. It was clear enough to him, if not to his counselors, that wealth and power are liabilities in the quest for love. He knew that any woman in the world would accept his proposal, for fear, if not for greed. But it wasn't *any* woman he wanted, for *any* reason. He desired a specific woman, and only for love.

Her name was Charisa. So beautiful was she that the king could never forget her after that one summer day, when, for just a few seconds, their eyes had met. Surrounded by his royal entourage, he had passed through her village on a long journey through his realm. There she stood amid the cheering crowd of revering subjects, silent and staring, no cheer on her lips, as he passed by.

"Why does she not cheer, or at least smile?" he wondered to himself. "Is she one of those who believe the dark rumor?"

He must know all about her. For three summers and two winters, Mashal acquainted himself with Charisa from a silent, secret distance. Sending trusted agents from his court to her village, they observed her daily life and asked questions of her fellow townspeople. So the king came to know Charisa and loved her more and more. But how could he ever approach her? As the days and nights passed by, nothing brought Mashal greater anguish than the thought that this one he loved so deeply might yield her hand to him either out of desire for his wealth or from fear of his power, or worse yet, from fear of the dark rumor. How could he ever really know if his bride had married for love? Indeed, how could she even know for sure? Alone he remained in this haunting agony.

Then one day a strange and hopeful idea came to him.

"If only I could somehow conceal my identity as king while yet revealing my heart, hiding my power and wealth, while making known my love . . ."

"That's it!" he exclaimed to himself. "That is the only way. I must devise a plan to conceal myself and yet reveal myself. If Charisa were to fall in love with me knowing only my heart, then I would know that her love was free and true."

Mashal immediately began to lay plans for his concealment. First, he selected a name.

"I shall be called Chaphas Galah, for I shall be concealed to reveal."

He laid claim to a trade.

"I shall be a craftsman in wood and stone, for I long to build love in Charisa by the revelation of my love for her."

Upon his well-trimmed head he grew dark brown locks to shoulder length. Upon his clean-shaven face a beard was let to grow. Laying aside his kingly robes, Mashal dressed himself in the clothes of a commoner. Then he saddled an old horse and rode as Chaphas into Charisa's village. Here he would make his home and seek the affections of her whom he had loved so long in secret.

As the days passed, Chaphas plied his trade among the people and became their friend. No one suspected his true identity. The concealment was effective. Finally, the day came when, in the natural course of village life, Charisa and Chaphas met for the first time. The place of encounter was the open market in the village square. Mutual attraction was immediate.

"She is more lovely than I remember," he whispered under his breath.

"His eyes are strangely familiar," she thought to herself. "Such kind eyes."

"Hello, my name is Chaphas. May I make your acquaintance?"

"I am Charisa. Are you new to our village?"

So began the tryst of this common maiden of rare beauty and this concealed king of singular power, immense wealth and dark rumor. Unfolding before them were days and weeks and months of growing fondness and friendship. Casting to learn her feelings, one day Chaphas suggested that perhaps they would be more than friends in time. Charisa smiled to let him know that her heart was tending in the same direction.

Chaphas was hopeful that Charisa was falling in love with him, and he was certain he was falling more in love with her.

Then came an unexpected pain, piercing his tender heart like the sharp arrow from an enemy's bow. One day as the two of them talked and laughed and explored one another's heart, Charisa confided to Chaphas that she believed the dark rumor about the king.

Trying to hide his sinking disappointment, hesitant yet curious, Chaphas inquired, "*Why* do you believe the rumor? I don't."

"I know it to be true, for a reason I cannot reveal to anyone, not even you, Chaphas . . . not yet."

"Besides," she continued, "I once saw the king. He looked straight at me through the cheering crowd, and the rumor glared true in his eyes. All that my father . . . I mean . . . all that my friends have told me of the king's dark heart was clear enough in his countenance."

Chaphas was silent for a moment.

"How could it be," he wondered with sadness, "that she could have seen what was not true in my eyes, and see not the same now as I become her love, for my eyes are the same in my concealment?"

If we could have spoken to Mashal, we would have told him that there is no mystery here, for we all see what we believe we will see, true or not. She saw an enemy in the king because she was told she would see an enemy, and she believed the one who had told her.

"Your father?" Chaphas probed. "Did you say your father told you the dark rumor?"

"No!" Charisa firmly denied, her eyes shifting to the horizon beyond his shoulder. "I said my friends told me."

It's not that Charisa didn't want to tell Chaphas about her father. She had been longing for years to know someone dearly enough to tell. But she knew now that she truly loved Chaphas with all her heart. And she feared that rejection would follow if he knew the heavy secret she carried in her heart, especially since he did not believe the rumor.

But now Chaphas *did* know her secret, for in that slip of the tongue about her father, a familiar resemblance came over her countenance. The shock stabbed deep within him.

"Tell me," he demanded, "for I have seen the truth in your eyes. Tell me your father's name."

Realizing that she must tell, and somewhere in her heart wanting to tell, Charisa risked the ruin of the only true love she had ever known.

"Kazab," she blurted out with trembling. "I am the daughter of Kazab, the great warrior king, now in exile by the hand of Mashal. There, you know. Now you will surely hate me for my secret, but I know the dark rumor about King Mashal is true."

Oh, how fierce the conflict raged in his torn and bleeding heart!

And yet . . . and yet . . . he could not refrain from loving her.

Though she was birthed into the arms of his only true enemy . . .

Though she was raised and educated in the dark rumor about himself . . .

Though she believed the lie and hated him for it . . .

Though the truth of her evil parentage and deceived plight be ever so low, he could not, for he would not, cease loving her. If only he could free her from the dark rumor's influence, then perhaps she could bear to know his true identity and still love him.

There was one ray of hope to which he clung. While she hated him, the king, she also loved him, the common man. In loving Chaphas, she loved Mashal. For although in Chaphas the king's power was concealed, truly his heart was revealed. It was the heart of the king she loved, though she knew it not.

Chaphas embraced Charisa's trembling body and wiped the tears from her cheeks. He whispered, "There are many things I want to tell you, but you cannot bear them now. But be assured, I love you still."

She wondered, but rested in his unfailing love.

Here then was the task before him: to reveal to her that all the goodness she loved in Chaphas was the truth about the king. Yea more, that the one she loved was in fact the king.

And what a delicate matter it would be! To simply make an abrupt declaration of his true identity might make him appear a lunatic in her eyes, if she believed him not. Or she might feel his goodness and love to be part of the charade which had concealed his true identity. A delicate matter indeed!

There were still two vital certainties in his favor. He knew the full truth about her, and still loved her just the same. He was no lunatic, nor a twisted pretender. He became Chaphas not because he was a king of power and dark rumor, but a king in love.

With firm resolve, he set his course.

"I will keep on loving her as Chaphas," said the king in his heart, "and then, when finally I am revealed to be the king, she will know in that moment of disclosure that my love is true and the dark rumor is a lie. She will see that I had both known her as an enemy and yet loved her as my dearest friend."

The four seasons passed—winter, spring, summer, autumn—and the identity of Chaphas was not yet known to Charisa's mind. But his love was known yet more to her heart. Trust deepened. Loyalty strengthened. The capacity to even imagine life without Chaphas faded from her heart until she felt they were forever one. They spoke freely of their coming betrothal and agreed that when they married the wedding would be among his family and friends in the city from which he came.

One day as they walked hand-in-hand amid the changing colors of autumn woods, Chaphas sensed that the time for another change was approaching.

"Charisa, my love," Chaphas spoke with trembling tone, "there is more to tell of myself that you must know, and I hope you will love me still."

Charisa broke in with extreme confidence, "I know your heart and that is enough, precious love of my only dream. Nothing you can tell could ever diminish my love for you, for even your secret must reveal yet more of the goodness that makes you so desirable in my eyes."

"Soon enough you will know my secret, but first, the question that consumes my heart day and night. Will you, Charisa, be my wife?"

"Yes, yes, a thousand times yes," she eagerly responded.

"Then it is decided," said Chaphas. "We will make the journey to my homeland and there we will be married."

The village folks rejoiced to hear the news and bade the happy couple farewell.

It was the perfect time of year to make the long journey before them. On horseback they traveled by day at no hurried pace, stopping to enjoy the beauties of the country along the way. Playing in waterfalls, gathering wild flowers, reposing in quiet valleys, they soared still higher in one another's love.

Finally, nearing journey's end, Chaphas pointed with Charisa's arm outstretched under his, "There, that is my city in the distance."

As they drew closer, occasional travelers from the city met them on the road and bowed low before them.

"What kind of greeting is this for such as you and I?" Charisa inquired.

"All will be clear very soon, my love."

Entering the city gates, they were met with shouts of gladness and cheering fit for a king and queen. Charisa's perplexity deepened. She looked to Chaphas for understanding.

Dismounting from their horses, Chaphas took her hand in his and led her up a massive stairway into the palace.

"Where are we, Chaphas," Charisa solemnly demanded.

"We are home, my queen-to-be; that is, if, knowing me as I am, you still love me."

In the next moment, like a flash of light, painful yet illuminating, the picture became clear in Charisa's mind. She began to weep.

"You are the king," she responded with amazement. "That was your secret."

"You are under no obligation," Mashal urged with sincerity. "My love is forever yours, if you choose to have it. If not, though it would bring me great pain, you are free to go."

"Free to go?" Charisa spoke through her tears. "I am free, and yet I am the willing captive of your love. You knew me as Kazab's daughter, you knew I hated you, but you loved me still. The dark rumor, then, is a lie, for I know your love to be true."

Thus it was that Mashal Melek Attiq, King of Ancient Power, and Charisa, lady of grace, became husband and wife in the Land of Emeth, which being interpreted means, Land of Truth. For true love knows no power but love alone.

So our story comes to an end, and a happy end at that. And yet it is not the end. If you close your eyes and pray for understanding, you will see your own place in the story.

— *Chapter Ten* —

Love's Downward Ascent

INCARNATION

The butterfly entered the cocoon
And emerged a lowly caterpillar,
Never again to fly.
So backwards,
So radically,
Beautifully backwards!

I MAGINE THE unimaginable.

One moment He was there, and had always been there for all eternal ages past. They were together, as they had ever been. The next moment He was gone, and the very shape of God's reality was forever and radically changed. An aching chasm of separation now lay between them. The Godhead itself would never again be the same.

The intimate friendship of the Father, Son and Holy Spirit is a wonder too high for us to ever fully comprehend. I have had the incredible privilege of loving a girl named Sue, and being loved by her, for twenty-two years. I know from personal experience that love is exponential, capable of ceaseless growth, with no apparent plateau. It is always possible to love more, with greater intensity and deeper satisfaction. As far as I can see, love is a reality of infinite dimensions. I expect that Sue and I will forever soar higher in our friendship. And to think, this has been our experience with the hindering liabilities of sin and its various effects of "disfunctionality" upon us. So imagine the pure passion and high fidelity of the love that has always existed between the Father, Son and Holy Spirit, within the utterly perfect environment of their sinless fellowship. If love is infinitely expansive in its capacity for development in the lives of created beings like you and me, perhaps we could say God exists at love's vanishing point, where its horizon ever recedes to a never-ending beyond of more and yet more love. And yet, that vanishing point must only present itself to *our* perception as we approach. For God, there can be no vanishing point because love is not something He taps into as a power external to Himself. God *is* love. The totality of love—its infinite, immeasurable whole—has its unborrowed source in Him. He never experiences *more* love, but always is Himself *all* love. So it may be more accurate to say that God exists at love's zenith point, which to us is always the vanishing point.

Whatever the case may be, we say all we can of this infinite love, and then we stand back in breathless amazement as we watch God the Son depart from that holy, eternal fellowship to become one with the fallen human race. All the Son had ever known was the intimacy of face-to-face, heart-to-heart friendship with the Father and the Holy Spirit. When He suddenly, at the appointed time, vanished into the starry expanse beyond, all of heaven was silenced. A hush of wonder blanketed the angels, for "these are things that angels long to see into" (1 Peter 1:12, NEB). They could only whisper with astonishment, "Where has He gone . . . our Creator and Friend?" And yet they knew His chosen destiny was our death-stricken world. But it was too much to speak, so they asked the question with no need for an answer.

A prophetic ear once heard an angel cry out, "Think ye that the Father yielded up His dearly beloved Son without a struggle? No, no. It was even a struggle with the God of Heaven, whether to let guilty man perish, or to give His beloved Son to die for him" (*Early Writings,* p. 151). The angels watched and whispered as God's love unfolded in our salvation. They were witnesses to the divine struggle.

Can we even conceive of omnipotent, omniscient God going through a struggle? Does our picture of the Almighty forbid us to see that God's heart is capable of pain, even the pain of intense struggle to let go of His most cherished companion in order to continue loving His rebellious enemies above Himself? If we can't see it, then our picture of God is fatally flawed, and the cold, passionless conception we idolize as God will inevitably make us cold and passionless ourselves.

God emerged from that desperate travail determined to save you and me at any cost to Himself. And what a cost it would be! The Son departed from the tender embrace of His Father. He who had always been present to the Godhead and all the angelic host suddenly disappeared from all heavenly sight and touch, descending into the confinement of a teenage girl's womb. There, as an embryo, cell by cell, God the Son was reconstructed of our flesh and bone and blood. He remained God—how could He not?—and yet He literally became a human being. The Creator became the created.

Down.

It's the direction none of us want to go. And for good reason, or so we think. For is it not obvious that to go down is to lose, and don't we want to win? To go down is to descend low, and certainly we want to rise high. To be weak, and don't we want to be strong? Down is clearly not the way anyone should choose to go, is it? Is it not the wrong way?

And yet, there is something more to *down* than meets the eye at first glance. After all, we are confronted with a bewildering and disconcerting fact. He who occupied the very highest position in the universe went down, not by force or defeat, but by choice. It makes absolutely no sense to our natural way of thinking. That's why Paul calls it a "mystery," not because God is deliberately hiding it from us, but because we don't get it. To our *irrational* rationality, willing condescension is "foolishness" (1 Corinthians 1:18-25).

But that's exactly what God did in Christ. He willingly chose to descend to the very lowest place in all the universe. Trace those seven downward steps in the words of Paul:

"Christ Jesus . . . being in very nature God,
did not consider equality with God
Something to be grasped,
But made Himself nothing,
Taking the very nature of a servant,
Being made in human likeness.
And being found in appearance as a man,
He humbled Himself
And became obedient to death—
Even death on a cross!
Therefore God exalted Him to the highest place
And gave Him the name that is above every name,
That at the name of Jesus every knee should bow,
In Heaven and on earth and under the earth,
And every tongue confess that Jesus Christ is Lord,
To the glory of God the Father" (Philippians 2:5-11, NIV).

Here is the consummate revelation of the true heart and mind of God. Here is how utterly selfless and other-centered is His love. No playacting! God the Son literally did not regard His position of equality with God the Father to be of greater value than our salvation. He would rather give up the totality of Himself and cease even to live at all, than to let us perish in our sin. The thought of such sacrifice makes us want to shout, "No, don't do it!" And yet, there was no stopping Him. With no self-centered calculation, and no risk-free guarantee of return, He moved from His high throne to the edge of our dark night. Unhesitatingly, He plunged full force into a free-fall of self-abandonment into the deepest depths of our sin and guilt.

Down . . .

    Down . . .

        Down He descended.

Laying aside "His prerogatives as God's equal" (Philippians 2:6-7, Phi), He took up our liabilities and limitations as fallen human beings.

No longer omniscient, He had to acquire knowledge, to learn and to grow in understanding as we do, totally dependent on the Father.

"The Child continued to grow and become strong, increasing in wisdom" (Luke 2:40, NASB; see also Mark 13:32; John 10:18).

No longer omnipotent, He could only do what any other man or woman could do through faith in the Father.

"I can of Myself do nothing" (John 5:30).

"Jesus of Nazareth, a Man attested by God to you by miracles, wonders, and signs which *God did through Him* in your midst" (Acts 2:22).

No longer omnipresent, He was confined to a single human body, incapable of space transcendence.

"Jesus said to her, 'Do not cling to Me, for I have not yet ascended to My Father'" (John 20:17).

All that was *self* to Christ—abilities, powers, privileges, even His own life—all of Himself, but love alone, was willingly cast aside as He fixed His devoted eyes upon you and me. The very same love that had been the eternal pulse of the Trinity bled forth in the incarnation of God in Christ, making us the objects of that love in the most intimate sense.

How intimate? (Take a deep breath.)

In Christ, God is forever one with the human race. The incarnation brought about an eternal change for God. In a very real sense, He laid aside His own existence and took up ours. He was God, and only God. Now He is God, and also man. He is one with us in the closest possible way—by actual identity, by sameness, by brotherhood.

There is no indication in Scripture that God's becoming human was a temporary arrangement. Jesus did not lay aside His humanity after the cross. He rose from the grave as much "the Son of man" as He went into the grave. He died God-as-man and rose God-as-man. Deity became a human being in Christ forever. Our humanity is a permanent, eternal reality for Him.

And yet, while taking upon Himself our humanity, He has not ceased to be God, a fully divine member of the Trinity. This presents to our minds an astounding truth. In the victory and exaltation of Christ to the right hand of the Father, humanity is included.

Paul explains (read slowly):

"God, who is rich in mercy because of His great love with which He loved us, even when we were dead in trespasses, made us alive together with Christ (by grace you have been saved), and raised us up together, and made us sit together in the heavenly places in Christ Jesus" (Ephesians 2:4-6).

"In union with Christ Jesus He raised us up and enthroned us with Him in the heavenly realms" (NEB).

"For in Him the whole fullness of Deity (the Godhead) continues to dwell in bodily form [giving complete expression of the divine nature]. And you are in Him, made full and having come to fullness of life [in Christ you too are filled with the Godhead—Father, Son and Holy Spirit]" (Colossians 2:9-10, AB).

As unbelievable as it may seem, according to the apostle Paul, humanity has been incorporated into the Godhead by virtue of the incarnation of God the Son. Stepping down from the throne of the universe, God grafted our very human nature into the Trinity, creating an eternal, indissoluble union. He was born, He lived, He died, He was resurrected, and then ascended to resume His place in the Godhead, all while retaining our humanity. Not only did He come down to where we are, He lifted us up to where He is. "God was manifested in the flesh . . . received up in glory" (1 Timothy 3:16). Hence, Paul says we are enthroned at the Father's right hand in the divine-human person of Christ Jesus. We have been given a place in God's universe just short of divine. To be sure, we are no more than human, not in any sense made divine by this stunning arrangement. Our essential identity is not changed. But His is. He who was fully and only God has become just as fully man. He is our "head" and we are His "body" (Ephesians 1:22-23), because we are what He now is—human. Our exaltation in Christ is sheer grace upon us, and sheer sacrifice upon Him.

Let it never escape our enthralled notice that the incarnation of Christ was the incarnation of God. God, not someone else, became human. Not an angel nor any other created being, but God Himself. Therefore, we may speak with certainty and awe of *the humanity of God*. He is still God, and never ceased to be God. But now, He is as fully and literally human as He is God, and will be forevermore. Of God's relation to humanity it is written, "He is not ashamed to call them brethren" (Hebrews 2:11).

In Christ we encounter the glorious paradox of high and low, and we find it difficult to distinguish which we are seeing. What may appear a contradiction to our sin-tainted minds is in reality no contradiction at all, but rather a paradoxical harmony. The highest place in the universe just happens to be the lowest place as well. Love serves others above self with genuine, non-calculating interest. It is an extremely low position, but the very highest position to be had. And that's where God lives, at the place of high humility and lowly glory.

But God's law of condescending love is under siege.

There are presently two mysteries at war in the universe: (1) "the mystery of godliness," and (2) "the mystery of iniquity" (1 Timothy 3:16; 2 Thessalonians 2:7, KJV). Let us notice the difference between the two.

Paul points out that the "the mystery of iniquity" finds expression in "the man of sin, the son of perdition; who opposeth and exalteth himself above all that is called God" (2 Thessalonians 2:3-4, 7, KJV).

What is the mystery here? Is it not that in exalting himself Satan, and all who follow this mystery to its conclusion, are destined for "perdition"? It seems contradictory to our natural minds, but striving to exalt self is the recipe for self-destruction. To quest upward in self-centered determination produces a descending effect. "For whoever exalts himself will be humbled" (Luke 14:11).

Remember Philippians 2:5-11? In that remarkable passage Paul traces the condescension of Christ to the low place of incarnation and death, only to be exalted to the highest place in the universe. Notice this contrasting, parallel description of Lucifer's fall:

"How you are fallen from Heaven, O Lucifer, son of the morning! How you are cut down to the ground, you who weaken the nations! For you have said in your heart: 'I will ascend into Heaven, I will exalt my throne above the stars of God; I will also sit on the mount of the congregation on the farthest sides of the north; I will ascend above the heights of the clouds, I will be like the Most High.' Yet you shall be brought down to Sheol, to the lowest depths of the Pit" (Isaiah 14:12-15).

The subject of this fascinating Scripture is how Lucifer has "fallen" and gone "down." Strangely enough, or perhaps not so strangely now that we're beginning to understand how things work in God's universe, Lucifer ends up "down" by attempting to "ascend" up, by aiming to "exalt" himself and achieve a position "above" all others. By trying to occupy the highest place, he will be "brought down . . . to the lowest depths of the Pit."

Lucifer imagined that he could live better without love, that he could put himself first and thereby be first, that he could exalt himself and thereby be exalted. No such possibility exists, for the way up is, in fact, down. To descend in love and service for others above self is the only true way to ascend. This is what the Bible calls "the mystery of godliness," the secret power of God's character.

"Without controversy great is the mystery of godliness: God was manifested in the flesh [and] . . . received up in glory" (1 Timothy 3:16).

What is the mystery here? Is it not that in descending down in self-sacrificing love Christ is lifted up to the heights of glory? At His birth, the angels recognized His descent to the *lowest* place as "Glory to God in the *highest*" (Luke 2:14). As previously quoted, Philippians 2:5-11 traces the condescending steps in the sacrifice of Christ only to radically change directions: "Christ . . . made Himself nothing. . . . Therefore God exalted Him to the highest place."

Can you imagine being God and not regarding your position as something to be held onto? Of course you can't. Neither can I. But this is exactly what we see in Christ.

The mystery of godliness is the secret power that resides in God's character. That mystery is self-sacrificing love. God would rather make Himself nothing than allow you and me to be eternally lost. And yet, the mystery of this love is that it ascends even as it descends. It is a lowliness so low that it loops around to the highest place, like traveling the earth so far south that you end up at the North Pole. The act of making Himself nothing shows that He is truly something. The highest place in the universe happens to be the lowest place. The gospel teaches us that *the way up is down*. To willingly descend in self-forgetful love for others produces an ascending effect, though no such aim is the motive. Love is its own end. Honor and exaltation are its natural result, but not its quest. It is in the heart of God to go downward in service to others. He is infinitely humble. And we love and adore Him for being such a person, such an incredible God.

God wins by losing, by submitting to our hate, by not resisting our raging war against Him, "Who, when He was reviled, did not revile in return; when He suffered, He did not threaten" (1 Peter 2:23). And yet, in losing He cannot lose, for "the goodness of God leads [us] to repentance" (Romans 2:4). We are broken to pieces as we beat violently upon the unbreakable reality of His love for us. Exhausted and defeated, we end up worshiping Him through our tears. He wins because He continues to love us in the face of our hate.

God gains by giving, though gaining is never the point of His giving. He gives all that He has and all that He is, but is never depleted. Because love "does not seek its own," therefore "love never fails" (1 Corinthians 13:5, 8). It is impossible for love to ever cease or diminish because it is the very nature of love to grow and expand as it is given away. It regenerates, replenishes and enlarges as it flows outward. Jesus said it like this, as He contemplated the unfolding secret of His incarnation, "Anyone who holds on to life just as it is destroys that life. But if you let it go, reckless [selfless] in your love, you'll have it forever, real and eternal" (John 12:25, TM).

Did I say at the beginning of this chapter that the very shape of God's reality was forever and radically changed when Christ became a man? Now we're prepared to make one qualification: His inmost heart never changed. His essential core remained the same. In fact, that's why everything else did change. It was the very changelessness of His love that moved Him so passionately to change on our behalf.

The caterpillar is still a butterfly on the inside.

— *Chapter Eleven* —

Closer Than Angels
DESTINY

By angel tongues is spoken a truth,
    With hushed, astonished tone:
"The fallen race is God's bride,
    Destined for the throne."

THE BRIDE OF a king is queen. By virtue of their matrimonial union, all the wealth and authority of the kingdom belong to her as well as to him. And yet, if she married for love, all this is nothing compared to the joy of knowing the king as her lover and friend. She is first his beloved bride, then she is the queen.

What you are about to read will no doubt seem like a gross exaggeration. So be it. Such is the nature of true love. It always excels beyond necessity into the far reaches of extravagance. So go ahead and believe the unbelievable, if you dare.

Our purpose in this chapter is best served by first sketching a broad picture of our universe as a place populated by various orders of rational creatures. Then we will consider our privileged position within that structure.

We find in Scripture hints of the identity of the very first sentient being ever made by God. We also find clues as to who God created last. And in this tale of truth, both light and dark, we find that the first shall be last and the last shall be first.

Put the pieces together with me.

The book of Job, the most ancient inspired literature in our possession, calls our attention to the existence of non-human races that inhabit the cosmos beyond earth. In this particular passage, God is speaking to Job of the time and event of our world's creation. Listen carefully:

"Where were you when I laid the foundation of the earth? . . . When the morning stars sang together, and all the sons of God shouted for joy?" (Job 38:4, 7).

The first thing we notice here is chronology. Whoever these beings are, they predate the creation of earth and the human order, for they were joyous witnesses of our coming to be.

Second, it seems we have two categories before us: (1) "the morning stars" and (2) "all the sons of God."

The identity of the "sons of God" is a quickly solved mystery, and it is helpful to know who they are in our story. Earlier in Job, we have this intriguing record:

"Now there was a day when the sons of God [there they are] came to present themselves before the Lord, and Satan also came among them. And the Lord said to Satan, 'From where do you come?' So Satan answered the Lord and said, 'From going to and fro on the earth, and from walking back and forth on it'" (Job 1:6-7).

This assembly is convening in God's presence. Travel has occurred to bring the meeting together. Those who are present "came" from other locations in the universe where they live. They are identified as "the sons of God." While there is a sense in which all whom God has made are His children, there is a unique sense in which the title is used here. The genealogy of Jesus in the gospel of Luke helps us understand. Each person mentioned in the family tree is identified as the "son" of a particular human father: "David, the son of Jesse, the son of Obed, the son of Boaz," and so on the list goes. Back, back, back until we read, "Cainan, the son of Enosh, the son of Seth, the son of Adam, the son of God" (Luke 3:31-32, 37-38).

While all humans are the sons of God in the secondary sense of procreation, Adam alone had no human parents. He was "the son of God" in the primary sense, not born of any human lineage. He was himself the progenitor of the human race. As such, he is our father and "the son of God," established by the Creator as the head of this world.

But our world, Planet Earth with its human race, is not the only world God created. Hebrews 1:2 informs us that God made "worlds," plural. Revelation 12:12 addresses the "heavens, and you who dwell in them." The universe is inhabited. Ours is just one of many populated spheres. Paul further fills out the picture for us by announcing that there are "rulers and authorities in the heavenly places" (Ephesians 3:10, NASB). At least two things are clear from this insight: (1) the universe is populated with beings who live in actual "places" beyond earth, and (2) those populations operate in a structured, orderly manner, for where there are "rulers and authorities," there must be realms in which groups of individuals are organized and led.

It stands to reason that if Adam was called "the son of God" in a special sense due to his headship over the human race, then the "rulers" of the other worlds must also be "the sons of God" as heads of their various realms. Therefore, when Job 1:6 says, "there was a day when the sons of God came to present themselves before the Lord," we are witnessing a heavenly council meeting between God and the various leaders of all the worlds He has made. It makes sense, then, for Satan to answer God's challenging question as to his point of origin by saying he had come "from . . . the earth" (verse 7). This statement implies that the others attending the meeting are there as representatives of other planets, for Satan lays claim to this earth as the world he represents, and on that basis he urges his right to be present in this heavenly assembly.

Having identified "the sons of God" who pre-existed the human race, let us now turn our attention to "the morning stars" mentioned in Job 38:7.

Revelation 1:20 and 12:4 employ "stars" to symbolize an order of beings called "angels." The word *angel* means "messenger." If God's universe is a vast array of inhabited worlds, it makes sense for this enormous kingdom to be networked by means of some communication system. Numbering in the multiplied millions (Daniel 7:10), the angels fill this vital role. They are ambassadors, traversing the universe on missions of communication for God. As such, they reside in the immediate presence of the Creator, and are by this appointment the highest order in God's government, at least for a period of time.

The book of Job not only calls the angels *stars*, but "morning stars." And among the morning stars was one of special title and position. His name was "Lucifer," a name that means "son of the morning" (Isaiah 14:12). The usage here of the word *morning* does not refer to any and every morning, but indicates the very dawn of creation itself—the very first morning, as it were. As morning stars, it would appear that the angels are the first order of rational, free creatures ever made by God, and Lucifer was the first among them to come forth from the Creator's hand. He is the son of creation's morning light, the most ancient of all creatures.

Ezekiel adds insight to Lucifer's identity and position:

"Thou sealest up the sum, full of wisdom, and perfect in beauty" (Ezekiel 28:12, KJV).

The idea here is that Lucifer was created as the sum total of angelic perfection. As such, he was perhaps the model or pattern after which all the others were fashioned.

If our conclusion is correct regarding Lucifer being the first created being, then every other angel awoke to existence to meet him as the one closest to God and their appointed head. This helps to explain how and why fully one third of the angels, beings of incredible intelligence, followed Lucifer in his revolt against God (Revelation 12:4, 7). He was their leader by God's ordaining. He was their senior in age, having been created first. He was closest to God of all created beings. He was utterly perfect, the sum total of all charm, likeability and wisdom (Ezekiel 28:12). If anyone knew God, Lucifer did. If anyone could weave lies about God and be persuasive, Lucifer could. And he did, as we will now explore. First, I'd like to suggest a motive for the crime.

The chronology revealed in Job 38:7 indicates that Planet Earth, with its human race, was the final piece of the universe envisioned by God. Lucifer and the angelic order were created first. Then came "all the sons of God" and their various planets and populations. The human order, Adam and Eve and their posterity, came last. But as the creation unfolded to completion, it became obvious to all, including Lucifer, that while the human race was indeed last, it would not be at all least in God's plan. Humanity was the grand finale of Creation, the crown set atop the head of all God had made, and was intended to be His companion in the most intimate sense.

Here's where you need to brace yourself and take a deep breath. What we are about to discover is so truly incredible that you may find it hard to believe.

Contemplating the identity of the human race, King David wondered, "What is man that You are mindful of him, and the son of man that You visit him?" (Psalm 8:4). In answer to this question, the Holy Spirit inspired David to write, "You have made him a little lower than the angels, and You have crowned Him with glory and honor" (Psalm 8:5).

In the New Testament, the apostle Paul quotes this passage from David and adds one extremely significant feature to the picture:

"Thou hast made him [mankind] *for a little while* lower than the angels" (Hebrews 2:7, NASB). Remember, at this point, that the angels and all the sons of God were witnesses to the unfolding drama of man's creation.

Paul's insertion of the words, "for a little while," communicates the idea that man's position below the angelic order was a temporary arrangement in God's larger plan. If I say to you, "I will stay in this room," I could stay in this room forever. But if I say to you, "I will stay in this room for a little while," I have said, in effect, that there is a point in time when I will leave this room. Human beings were not created to occupy a permanent position in God's plan below the angels, but rather to eventually move beyond the angels in closeness of relation to God.

There are three biblical truths that add conceptual texture to Paul's bold statement about the high destiny of mankind above the angels: (1) inheritance, (2) enthronement, and (3) marriage.

Inheritance

It comes as no surprise to us that Jesus Christ is "the heir of all things" (Hebrews 1:2). Certainly. Of course. He is the divine Son of God. But it is difficult for us to comprehend what could possibly be meant by biblical statements like these:

"He who overcomes shall inherit all things, and I will be his God and he shall be My son" (Revelation 21:7).

"The Spirit itself bears witness with our spirit that we are children of God, and if children, then heirs—heirs of God and joint heirs with Christ" (Romans 8:16-17).

When we read that Christ is heir of all things, we find ourselves envisioning Him possessing all the wealth and authority of the universe. When we read that redeemed human beings shall "inherit all things," we tend toward lessening "all things" to "some things." After all, how could it possibly mean what it says? We are mere fallen human beings, deserving of death. If God just spares our lives and gives us a planet to exist on, that would be more than enough.

But when we read that we are "joint heirs with Christ," there is no getting around the fact that the "all things" of our inheritance are the same "all things" of His inheritance. It is clear that God has an extremely lofty destiny in mind for the likes of you and me. And if you think it makes no logical sense, you're right. It doesn't add up, in the sense of God giving us what we deserve. But it makes perfect sense in the light of His grace. God has decided to go overboard in expressing His love for us, by literally giving us the entire universe in Christ.

Enthronement

If you think our inheritance is extravagant, what do you make of this biblical promise:

"To him who overcomes I will grant to sit with Me on My throne, as I also overcame and sat down with My Father on His throne" (Revelation 3:21).

When I read things like this, I don't know whether to laugh or cry. It's so mind-blowing, so deeply humbling and yet so affirming, to think that God actually intends to seat you and me on the very throne of Christ—the epicenter of all authority for God's vast eternal kingdom.

The same idea was revealed to the prophet Daniel:

"Then the kingdom and dominion, and the greatness of the kingdoms under the whole heaven, shall be given to the people, the saints of the Most High. His kingdom is an everlasting kingdom, and all dominions shall serve and obey Him" (Daniel 7:27).

Here is presented before our astonished minds a wonder too great for comprehension. Sovereign God has decided in His grace to grant redeemed humanity dominion over all "the kingdoms under the whole heaven," second only to Himself in the privilege of serving the needs of all creatures.

Jesus announced this grand design when He said, "Seek the kingdom of God . . . for it is your Father's good pleasure to give you the kingdom" (Luke 12:31-32). This promise is staggering if taken just as it reads. Pause to contemplate what is encompassed in this term, "the kingdom of God." You can compose a list as long as your arm or you can simply speak the two biblical words of our inheritance: "all things" (Revelation 21:7). When all is said and done in this great war between good and evil, everything that remains will be included in God's everlasting kingdom: unfallen angels numbering in the millions and unfallen worlds we have never imagined. It is this very kingdom, "the kingdom of God," that shall be given into our serving charge at His "pleasure," when at last we are enthroned with Christ.

According to Scripture, the angels surround God's throne and stand before it:

"His throne was a fiery flame, its wheels a burning fire. . . . A thousand thousands ministered to Him; ten thousand times ten thousand stood before Him" (Daniel 7:9-10). As a "covering cherub" (Ezekiel 28:16), Lucifer was once closer to the throne of God than all other angels. But while angels come ever so near the throne, redeemed human beings will, in some sense, occupy throne status with Christ. "We shall also reign with Him" (2 Timothy 2:12).

Whatever it means, we can be sure of one thing: to have such an honor conferred upon us is in no way a reflection of what we deserve, but rather of a love so humble and selfless that such an act could never detract from God's glory, but only magnify it the more.

Marriage

And yet, our inheritance and enthronement mean very little compared with the highest honor of all. The God of the universe has chosen the human race, you and me included, to be His bride. Listen to Him speak to your heart in earnest, whispered tones:

"I will make you my wife forever.

I will be honest and faithful to you.

I will show you my love and compassion.

I will be true to you, my wife.

Then you will know the Lord" (Hosea 2:19-20, GW).

God's intention to make us His eternal bride helps make sense of our enthronement and the enormity of our inheritance. The bride of a king is queen, and by virtue of this matrimonial tie, all the wealth and authority of the king belong to her as well. And yet, if she married for love, all of this is nothing compared to the friendship of her husband, the king. Love, not wealth and authority, is what God's plan for us is all about.

We are familiar with no more intimate relationship than marriage. God knows this, since we experience it by His own intentional design. He employs marriage as a symbol of the relationship He desires with us because He is calling our hearts to something very special, sacred, and monogamous with Himself.

When Elohim said, "Let us make man in Our image, according to Our likeness," He was writing a part of the creation drama unlike all chapters before. The human pair, and all their offspring, were designed to experience and reveal dimensions of divine love known only within the inner circle of the Trinity itself. Like Elohim, they would be an "us," male and female, two yet one, the most perfect reproduction of God's image. As such, they were created with the capacity to experientially engage in the deeper mystery of God's love between themselves on a level not possible for angels. And through that experience they were to grow into a maturity of love that would prepare them for intimacy with the triune God on the deepest level possible for created beings.

Of course, the angels were also made to live within the reality of God's selfless, other-centered love. Indeed, all created entities reflect that love to varying degrees of perfection. But the multilevel depth of God's love is a fathomless ocean of boundless enormity. While the simple flowers of the field reveal something about God, there is much they do not even begin to say. The animal kingdom describes more than the flower, and yet leaves a wealth of greater wonders unexpressed. The angels soar high above flowers and animals as complex, sentient creatures of breathtaking beauty and incredible wisdom. They not only reveal God's love, they experience it as they reveal it, as conscious, freewill creatures. And yet, there is more of God's love to be experienced and revealed. Human beings were created to reach the highest plane of experiential involvement with the divine heart, even to surpass the angels in nearness to God. Humanity was brought into existence to become the bride and queen of Elohim.

God is asking us to marry Him.

For love.

And yet, it is His highest pleasure to give us all the universe as well.

— *Chapter Twelve* —

"*Omnipassionate*"
Flame of Love
DIVINE EMOTION

Holy fire of love divine,
 Burning white with passion hot;
Ignite in me Your quenchless flame,
 Which all my life I've yearning sought.
Course consuming through my veins,
 Oh love that dies to ever give;
Crucify my self with Your self,
 Mysterious death! For yet I live.

THERE'S ONLY ONE other person I've ever kissed besides my wife, my kids and my mom . . . and, oops, I almost forgot Dr. Philip Samaan, Professor of Theology at Southern University. He deserved it, which he will shyly admit. But . . . shhh! Don't tell him I told you, because he specifically told me never to tell anyone, even though it was a biblical kiss (1 Thessalonians 5:26).

I didn't get her name, this only other one. But I'll never forget her as long as I live, which will be for eternity. She was staring at me from across the crowded theater foyer, where people were gathered to visit after a lecture I had just given. About 5'3" and 120 pounds. Dark brown eyes. And light colored hair. I mean really light, like grey. She was 86 years old. Mind you, I'm in my thirties. Plus, I'm married. She stared on, not realizing I had noticed her from the corner of my eye.

I casually looked her way and smiled.

She quickly turned away.

As I resumed talking with those nearest to me, I could feel her eyes upon me once more. Allowing her a moment to relax her guard, I abruptly glanced her way again with a smile, as if to say, "Ah ha. Caught ya."

She nervously shifted her eyes to the floor.

So I began to make my way through the crowd toward her. There she stood, back to a wall, all alone, body stooped slightly forward, hands in her coat pockets, visibly uneasy that I was approaching.

"Good evening, ma'am. I'm so glad you could attend the meeting tonight. I certainly hope it was a blessing."

"Oh, it was," she replied.

"Perhaps you have a question about the lecture or something you'd like to share with me?" I asked, placing my hand on her shoulder and giving a gentle squeeze to put her at ease.

To my surprise, she shook slightly as I touched her and began to cry, attempting to hold back the tears. Thinking I had perhaps given pain to an injured shoulder, I quickly removed my hand and apologized. Then she spoke words that are forever etched in my memory.

"No, don't apologize; it's me. I'm sorry. It's just that . . . well . . . no one has touched me in more than twelve years."

"What!"

I could hardly believe what I was hearing.

I recalled to mind the sick experiment conducted by Emperor Fredrick II of Germany in the thirteenth century. Curious to know what language children would naturally speak without any human influence (certain it would be German), the Emperor took a number of babies from their mothers at birth and isolated them. The nurses who cared for the infants were strictly forbidden to speak in their presence or even touch them. All changing, washing and feeding was performed with utensils. It was never discovered what language they would speak because all the babies died before even their first lisp. In 1248, the historian Salimbene wrote of the inhuman tampering, "They could not live without petting," meaning affectionate touch.

"Are you serious?" I incredulously asked the elderly woman as she wiped tears from her wrinkled cheeks, "No one has touched you in years?"

"Not since my husband died twelve years ago."

Then came the kiss. I couldn't help myself. Overcome by the moment, I planted one on the old lady.

"Do you like me or something?" she asked with a labored smile.

"Oh, no," I thought, "now I'm in trouble."

"No, ma'am," my tongue raced ahead of my brain. "I mean, yes. But I'm married . . . but I do like you . . . Hey, can I call you Grandma?"

"That's good to know," she replied. "It is so very good to know someone likes you. Thank you for liking me, and for touching me. I feel much better now."

This poor woman was withering away in her lonely isolation. Since her husband passed away she had been living alone in a one-room apartment, only occasionally walking to a nearby store to buy food. In the two weeks that followed, night after night she attended the meetings I was holding in the theater. Some of my friends and I continued to interact with her—talking and listening, smiling and laughing, touching her and liking her as a new friend. We had the privilege of watching her open up like a flower blossoming with new vitality. She became colorful and fragrant, confident and free.

Why are we like this? Why are we such emotional creatures, so needing to be touched and liked and loved?

I can think of but one reason: because we were made in the image of God. The only reason there are things like keys is because there are things like locks. The only reason there are things like shoes and gloves is because there are things like feet and hands. And the only reason we have emotions is because there is God, who is Himself the very epicenter of all pure emotion.

You have no doubt heard that there is a "God-shaped hole" in every human heart. It's true. He alone can satisfy our deepest desires. We need Him, or we perish. But have you ever considered that there might be a "human-shaped hole" in God's heart? I think there is.

Does that mean God needs us like we need Him? Well, not exactly. If we were to say God needs us, we could only mean something deeper than need—namely that He who is "all in all" and therefore has no need, has chosen to need us, which is really more like want than need. God *wants* us. He *desires* us, while not needing us as we need Him for actual meaning and survival. But why does He want us? There is only one answer to every question about God: "God is love." His desire for us is love in the form of grace.

Have you ever really thought about the emotional side of God? Aristotle, the ancient Greek philosopher, would have us believe that God is "the unmoved Mover," a concept he received from Plato. The idea is that God exercises absolute control over the affairs of men as the great "Mover" who causes all motion to occur; and yet, God Himself ever remains "unmoved," above and beyond any genuine interaction with created beings. Under the influence of these great Greek minds many Christian theologians describe God with the word *impassible,* meaning "incapable of feeling." It is rationalized that if God is absolutely perfect in knowledge and power, controlling all things by His Sovereign will and therefore knowing all things in advance, then, of course, He cannot actually respond to anyone outside of Himself. It is impossible, therefore, that God would be an emotional being, for it is the nature of emotion to emote, that is, to move; and to move means to change. If God were emotional, it is reasoned, then He would be less than perfect, less than God. If He is the Sovereign Ruler over every outcome, then He could never be affected or conditioned in His course of action by any influence external to Himself.

This view of God is quite cold and stoic, but its advocates claim that it elevates God to the high and holy place He belongs in our understanding, far above us with impassible grandeur and glory.

I'd like to suggest that the opposite is true. To view God as passionless does not elevate Him above us, but rather casts Him below us. God would, in fact, be greatly limited if He were incapable of moving in response to persons outside of Himself. But this is not the case. God does move. So far from being "the unmoved Mover," He is "the most passionate Mover" in all the universe. We are emotional because we were created in the image of God. The essence of the divine perfection is love, a love that continually moves out of itself to meet our needs.

By virtue of His love, God is extremely sensitive and attentive to those whom He has made to stand as free beings distinct from Himself. How else can we account for the numerous passages of Scripture that clearly tell us God does "change" His "mind" (Jeremiah 26:3), experience "regret" over decisions He has made (1 Samuel 15:10-11), "relent" or "repent" (Jeremiah 18:7-10; 1 Chronicles 21:15; Exodus 32:14), and modify His actions in response to human supplication (Exodus 4:10-15, 33:1-17; Deuteronomy 9: 13-29; Jonah 3:10; 4:2; 2 Kings 20:1-6)?

Someone will say, perhaps even you, that such biblical portrayals of God are too human to be taken just as they read. They are anthropomorphic images never intended to be taken as the literal truth about God. For God is God and, therefore, He cannot change, for change implies weakness or defect.

I beg to differ. Actually, certain kinds of change denote strength and reveal no defect. It is true that the Bible says God does not "change" (Malachi 3:6). With Him "there is no variation or shadow of turning" (James 1:17). "Jesus Christ is the same yesterday, today, and forever" (Hebrews 13: 8). But as we previously noted, the Bible also says that God does change in response to human need.

There is no contradiction here. Those passages that tell us God does *not* change are speaking of His essential character. God is love, and that reality is unalterable. But it is precisely because He is changeless in love that He is so fluid in His manner of relating to us. Those passages that speak of God changing do not refer to His character, but rather to His emotions and actions in response to our free choices.

If what you've been reading in this book has aroused in you a sense of discomfort or resistance, I understand. If it seems a bit overboard to think of God in terms of love and relationship and intimacy, you're not alone. I have the same reaction to the idea, and here I am writing about it. Truth be told, it is difficult to conceive of God as a person at all, let alone a passionate person with whom I could fall in love. And yet, this is exactly how Scripture portrays Him.

The Lord testified of King David, he is "a man after My own heart" (Acts 13:22). "He is a man whose heart beats to My heart" (TM). In David God saw a heart like His own, a heart with which He could resonate and beat in unison. This shepherd boy who became a king was a man of great strength who was in touch with the emotional side of his nature. He was a courageous king *and* a passionate poet. The most emotionally sensitive approaches to God in Scripture were penned by David's hand and sung by his lips:

"As the deer pants for the water brooks, so pants my soul for You, O God. My soul thirsts for God, for the living God. When shall I come and appear before God? . . . Deep calls unto deep at the noise of Your waterfalls; all Your waves and billows have gone over me. The Lord will command His lovingkindness in the daytime, and in the night His song shall be with me—a prayer to the God of my life" (Psalm 42:1-2, 7-8).

"O God, You are my God, earnestly I seek You; my soul thirsts for You, my body longs for You, in a dry and weary land where there is no water. I have seen You in the sanctuary and beheld Your power and Your glory. Because Your love is better than life, my lips will glorify You. I will praise You as long as I live, and in Your name I will lift up my hands. My soul will be satisfied as with the richest of foods; with singing lips my mouth will praise You. On my bed I remember You; I think of You through the watches of the night. Because You are my help, I sing in the shadow of Your wings. I stay close to You; Your right hand upholds me" (Psalm 63:1-8, NIV).

Not only are these the words of a man whose heart was beating in unison with God's own heart, these are words inspired by God. Not only are these David's sentiments toward God, but they are, in almost every respect, God's sentiments toward David, and toward you and me.

Also consider David's son, Solomon. He too was a man whose emotional floodgate was open toward God. The most passionate and, in some minds, debatable piece of literature in Scripture is the Song of Solomon. Why, may I ask, is this book in the Bible, if God is a being of absolute impassibility? Did the Holy Spirit really move in Solomon to inspire him to write such a "lovesick" (2:5) lyric to his girlfriend? Are these truly, in some real and deep sense, the thoughts and feelings of God coursing through the heart and pen of a man? The climax of the song would suggest not only that it is inspired by God, but that it is a prophecy of God's love that would become personified in the Messiah:

"Put me like a seal over your heart,
Like a seal on your arm.
For love is as strong as death,
Jealousy is as severe as Sheol;
Its flashes are flashes of fire,
The very flame of the Lord.
Many waters cannot quench love,
Nor will rivers overflow it;
If a man were to give all the riches of his house for love,
It would be utterly despised" (Song of Solomon 8:6-7, NASB).

Are you internalizing the significance of this lyric? The love that Solomon and his beloved bride-to-be felt for each other, as strong as death and burning with passion like flashes of fire, is here said to be "the very flame of the Lord." All of the true love we ever experience is part of the "fiery stream" that Daniel saw issuing "forth from before" the Lord (Daniel 7:9-10). The love of parent for child and child for parent, the love of best friends, and, yes, even the love that burns between a man and a woman, all have their origin in the "omnipassionate" heart of the omnipotent Three who are One in love.

Creation was movement on God's part. He reached out of Himself to make others with whom He could interact in dynamic, give-and-receive relationship. When the human race fell into sin, God was moved with grief and compassion, again reaching out of Himself to implement a plan by which to save us. The carrying out of that plan involved the most extreme divine movement. Embodied in the person of Jesus Christ we see the ultimate expression of God's emotions. The passion of Christ is the passion of God.

"He who has seen Me," Jesus declared, "has seen the Father" (John 14:9). The incarnation of God in Christ and His complete self-sacrifice on the cross forever prove that God is love—passionate, moving, selfless love. On the cross of Calvary the veil into God's heart was "torn in two from top to bottom" (Mark 15:38), exposing to our astonished gaze the depths of a love that would not let us go at absolutely any cost to Himself.

— *Chapter Thirteen* —

The Alluring
CROSS

Paradox for the blind,
    To open searching eyes;
See the veil, see behind,
    To hush your aching sighs . . .
        and answer lurking whys.

Paradox for the wise,
    To blind contriving sight,
See only the veil, imagine lies,
    See darkness, call it light . . .
        and chase eternal night.

My ALL-TIME favorite book title is *God in Search of Man,* by Abraham Joshua Heschel. The book is great, too. But the title alone is so bursting at the seams with significance. If ever a single phrase on the cover of a book spoke an entire volume of meaning to make the book itself seem superfluous, *God in Search of Man* does. If I had to choose just five words to describe the divine-human predicament, it would be those five. In one breath, this thoughtful Hebrew scholar has turned all our thinking about God and man on its head. So radically does this idea cut across our natural way of thinking that we feel as if we have just read something backwards. For we do, indeed, imagine the situation backwards: *Man in Search of God.* There, that sounds better. He is so distant, so aloof, so hard to find. And we, well, we are the noble pursuers of God, while He is the ignoble master of evasion.

Heschel slaps us upside the head and says, *Wake up to the reality that God is more passionately interested in us than we are in Him.* In actual fact, even our interest in Him is merely the returning echo of His in us.

God in Search of Man.

Ponder some of what is said in this simple declaration.

1. The first word is *God.* The last word is *Man.* A separation between God and man is explicit in the statement, for a search only occurs to recover what is not in one's possession.

2. That the separation is our choice and not God's is also clear, for God is the active pursuer.

3. The word *search* implies diligence on God's part, perhaps even desperation, and certainly energetic effort.

4. The fact that a search is necessary at all means that man is running or hiding from God in some way.

5. The fact that man is searched for by none other than God says that man is of extremely high value in God's eyes.

6. The fact that Almighty God is searching for evasive man suggests that God is holding the power of His sovereignty in reserve in favor of the power of persuasion, the attraction of His love.

7. That God would search for man by means of attraction rather than force confirms that God is desirous of recovering our loyalty while preserving our freedom, that He is aiming for relationship rather than control.

God in Search of Man—the divine search for you and me. Here is the whole truth. Everything else of meaning we have to say is expository to this one reality.

Listen as God groans with agony over the separation between Himself and us, and lean forward as He whispers His plan of pursuit:

She "'went after her lovers;
But Me she forgot,' says the Lord.
'Therefore, behold, I will allure her,
Will bring her into the wilderness,
And speak comfort to her'" (Hosea 2:13-14).
"See, now, I will be the One who attracts her,
And brings her into a desert place,
And speaks gently to her inmost heart" (Phi).
"I will win her back with words of love" (TEV).

These are truly stunning words to hear about ourselves from the Almighty. First notice that God designates Himself as a person distinct from us, and recognizes the grave magnitude of the freedom He has given us. "*You* forgot *Me*," He says. It is clear from this statement that God is a person who can and does feel the impact of our actions. By endowing us with free will, He ventured into the monumental risk that we might "forget" Him. And, tragically, we have. He also made Himself vulnerable to pain, which He now lives with as a perpetual reality since our falling out of love with Him.

Notice that God identifies Himself as our Lover, whom we "forgot" in order to pursue other "lovers."

Astounding!

What are we to make of this kind of language from our Creator? If He tells us He is our King to whom we owe allegiance, we easily grasp that picture and bow before Him. If He tells us He is a Warrior on a holy rampage against evil, we have no problem enlisting for the battle under Him. But when God tells us He is our Lover and pleads for the adultery to cease, when He asks for a restored relationship based on trust and love . . . well, then we find our hearts cold and distant. We sense the truth of our infidelity but are reluctant to admit that our situation could be all that bad. But it really is. Our sin is nothing less than adultery in God's eyes. "Oh shame, where is thy blush!"

How He chooses to respond to our sin reveals much about this One who identifies Himself as the Lover of our wayward souls.

"I will allure her," He proclaims His plan to save us.

So great is His love for you and me that He cannot let us go. And yet, He cannot coerce our loyalty. Refraining from the exercise of force or manipulation, He determines to "allure" our hearts away from all other lovers to Himself. It is evident that it is not control He seeks, but our free love based on who He is. An allurement is an attraction that catches the eye, a captivating beauty that wins the affections. Because the essence of our fallen condition is to live for self, we simply cannot see past ourselves without some kind of startling attraction of sufficient beauty to break the intoxicating infatuation. That alluring attraction is the cross of Christ. "And I, as I am lifted up from the earth [on the cross], will attract everyone to Me" (John 12:32, TM). In the experience of Jesus at Calvary we see the climactic revelation of our divine Lover's heart. He has chased after us into perilous territory, risking all in a desperate quest to arouse our love for Him by the manifestation of His own. Out of Himself He runs to find us, and His search has led Him to what Scripture calls "the sacrifice of Himself" (Hebrews 9:26).

Do not miss the significance of this breathtaking divine act. It does not say He sacrificed part of Himself, or much of Himself, or even most of Himself. It says He sacrificed "Himself," without qualification, which can only mean that He sacrificed the totality of Himself.

Contemplating the seriousness of the ordeal before Him, Jesus explained His struggle to the disciples:

"Now My heart is troubled—and what shall I say? Shall I say, 'Father, do not let this hour come upon Me?' But that is why I came—so that I might go through this hour of suffering. Father, bring glory to Your name!" (John 12:27, TEV).

Do you see the core issue Jesus is facing? As He feels the weight of our sin beginning to bear down upon His heart, He realizes that He is free to choose Himself over us. "Should I call upon My Father to deliver *Me* and abandon *them* to their guilty demise, or should I submit *Myself* to whatever suffering lies ahead in order to save *them?*" In answer to that struggle, all truth and beauty and love converged in a single decision. Jesus chose our eternal salvation over His own life. Dying upon the cross, absolutely free not to, God in Christ demonstrated beyond question that He values all others above Himself.

The alluring beauty of the cross lies in its demonstration of God's love. "By this we know love, because He laid down His life for us" (1 John 3:16). Here is the biblical definition of love. As we noted in a previous chapter, God is a triune personage who is both self and other. The constant motion of God is to be self and yet live for others. This core reality of the divine character is what Scripture calls *love*. When the Bible says, "God is love," it means *God is other-centered*. In order to save fallen humanity, God's love was extended to the farthest possible extreme: He literally "laid down His life."

In order for love to be anything of significance at all, it must be completely other-centered. Anything short of that would render it indistinguishable from sin itself. Faced with the choice, love could only choose the complete death of self for the life of any and all others, or it would have no meaning whatsoever. Even if God were to give all the wealth of the universe for our salvation, but refrain from giving Himself, His professed love would be proven a lie. "If a man would give for love all the wealth of his house, it would be utterly despised" (Song of Songs 8:7). Love's sacrifice must reach beyond the giving of things external *to* self to the giving of all that *is* self. If truly "love . . . does not seek its own" (1 Corinthians 13:5), then it must not seek its own to the nth degree of personal existence itself. If, as the Bible claims, the cross of Christ was a revelation of God's love, then we must witness there God staring into the dark abyss of complete annihilation, under no compulsion or obligation, and freely choosing that end rather than to let us perish without hope.

In Gethsemane and on the cross, Jesus made five revealing statements that open our understanding to the nature of His sacrifice on our behalf. It will be helpful to first take a sweeping aerial view of all five.

1. To Peter, James and John He said, "My soul is exceedingly sorrowful, even to death" (Matthew 26:38).

2. To the Father He Prayed, "O My Father, if it is possible, let this cup pass from Me; nevertheless, not as I will, but as You will" (Matthew 26:39).

3. In Gethsemane Jesus told Peter, "Don't you know that I could call on my Father for help, and at once He would send Me more than twelve armies of angels?" (Matthew 26:53, TEV).

4. To the Father He cried out, "My God, My God, why have You forsaken Me?" (Matthew 27:46).

5. To His Father He prayed, "Into Your hands I commit My spirit" (Luke 23:46).

These five statements reveal much, leading us through the progression of mental and emotional experience that transpired in Christ from deep darkness into triumphant light. The first one tells us that the suffering of our Savior was primarily the psychological weight of our sin. The second clearly shows that His sacrifice involved a decision to completely abandon Himself for our salvation, whatever the cost. The third statement informs us that His sacrifice was totally an act of love rendered in voluntary freedom. The fourth opens to our astonished sight just how real and dark and complete was the sacrifice. Finally, by committing His spirit to the Father Jesus indicated that He pierced through the darkness of death into the light of life by faith in the Father's love.

Now let's construct the picture with a little more detail.

When we see Jesus on the cross, terrible physical torture is evident. Hanging between heaven and earth, He was torn and bruised and bleeding. His breath was labored. Every tendon was wrenched as the weight of His body bore down upon the nails that were pierced through His hands and feet. What excruciating agony! And yet, "as a sheep before her shearers is silent, so He did not open His mouth" (Isaiah 53:7, NIV). Physical suffering prompted no word from the Savior's lips.

Silent while being tortured?

Why?

How?

An insightful line from *King Lear* says, "Where the greater malady is fixed, the lesser is scarce felt." Jesus was silent under physical abuse because the suffering imposed on His body with such vicious cruelty was a "lesser" pain "scarce felt" due to the greater agony transpiring deep in His inner soul.

"My soul is exceedingly sorrowful, even to death" (Matthew 26:38). Jesus spoke these words before any physical suffering had been inflicted upon Him. And yet, in Gethsemane He told the disciples that He was already dying—before reaching the cross. The Greek word here translated "soul" is *psyche*. It was not physical torture that took the life of Jesus. He suffered and died under the agonizing weight of a psychological torment so far exceeding bodily pain that it was nothing by comparison.

Isaiah foretold His suffering with these words:

"He was wounded for our transgressions . . . The Lord has laid on Him the iniquity of us all" (Isaiah 53:5-6).

"For He shall bear their iniquities . . . He poured out His soul unto death . . . and bore the sin of many" (Isaiah 53:11-12).

When Jesus condescended to become one with the fallen human race, it was a decision to bear the guilt of our sin as His own. We learned earlier in this book that the guilt imposed on our conscience by sin has erected a veil in our hearts to distort our vision of God's true character of love. Satan adds his accusing voice to the accusing of our own guilty conscience, trying to persuade us that God will not forgive. Jesus felt the full magnitude of our guilt and heard Satan's voice urging Him that God's love could not reach deep enough to pardon sinners. As our guilt bore down upon His psyche, for a period of time Jesus felt forever abandoned by the Father. The silence of the Infinite Sufferer was broken with the heart-rending cry, "My God, My God, why have You forsaken Me?" (Matthew 27:46). A deep sense of separation from God flooded His heart. His thoughts and feelings are clearly represented in this Messianic prophecy:

"I am abandoned among the dead;

I am like the slain lying in their graves,

Those You have forgotten completely,

Who are beyond Your help.

You have thrown Me into the depths of the tomb,

Into the darkest and deepest pit.

Your anger lies heavy on Me,

And I am crushed beneath its waves.

You have caused My friends to abandon Me;

You have made Me repulsive to them.

I am closed in and cannot escape" (Psalm 88:1-8, TEV).

"I am shut up, and I cannot come forth" (KJV).

The last line reveals just how dense the darkness became in our Savior's heart.

"Shut up."

"Closed in."

Where?

The context is clear. Jesus felt enclosed in "the darkest and lowest pit," "abandoned" to death as a sinner beyond hope. He felt "forgotten completely" by God, "crushed beneath" the waves of His "anger."

"I cannot come forth."

"Cannot escape."

Meaning what, exactly?

To "come forth" from death is resurrection. For a period of time, when the darkness was deepest, Jesus felt in His inner psyche that the separation between Himself and the Father would be eternal. "I am shut up, and I cannot come forth." The hope of resurrection was blocked from His view by our sin and guilt.

And yet, He did not call upon the Father for twelve legions of angels to deliver Him, as He clearly told Peter He could. This is crucial to our understanding. The will of Christ was absolutely free at every point in His sufferings. He was never trapped or made an unwilling victim. Every step of the way He maintained a conscious, freewill decision to continue loving us at any cost to Himself. There is only one possible way He could stare into the dark abyss of complete and final separation from the Father and not choose release. A power far greater than the fear of eternal death, far greater than any sense of self-interest or desire for life, was present and undying within His heart. That power was love. He literally loved you and me more than His own existence. While He *could* choose to escape in His sovereign freedom, He *would not* make that choice due to His love for our lives above His own.

But it is precisely because love knows only of complete self-sacrifice that it knows nothing of defeat. "Love never fails" (1 Corinthians 13:8). As the dark sense of separation from the Father enveloped His heart, Jesus reached through to the other side by faith. "Father," He prayed, "into Your hands I commit My spirit" (Luke 23:46), indicating a final resolve of confidence in His future with the Father. By trusting in the Father's good character, the Savior penetrated past the tormenting guilt of our sin, and past Satan's accusing voice, to believe He could fully rest in the Father's love. While at one point Jesus felt utterly forsaken, shut up in our death without the possibility of resurrection, His final prayer makes it clear that He emerged from the darkness victorious over sin's power to separate us from God. He fully expected to be with us and the Father in Heaven.

God in Christ descended to the lowest place of self-sacrifice, only to reveal a love that elevates Him high above every other conceivable attraction.

What matchless beauty!

What utterly selfless love!

"Draw me away!" (Song of Solomon 1:4).

"I sleep, but my heart is awake; it is the voice of my beloved! He knocks" (Song of Solomon 5:2).

I am allured.

Are you?

Chapter Fourteen

Not Master, But Husband

LAW

A mighty man with heavy hand,
    Subdued a woman's will;
"She is mine," he claimed the prize,
    But her heart resisted still.

Another with no force at all,
    Pursued with love alone;
"I am his," she yielded free,
    "My heart shall be his own."

RECENTLY I CONDUCTED an experiment to discover whether slavery is better than marriage. My hunch was that marriage is better, but I wanted to be absolutely sure. For an entire day, every time my wife asked me to do something—which, as it turns out, is more often than I thought—I answered, "Yes, Master."

The first few times she just gave me a weird look, because she knows I can be a little weird at times. I guess she thinks weird people deserve to be looked at weird. So be it. The experiment must go on.

By lunch she was visibly disturbed, but I was getting lots of stuff done. By bedtime, she slugged me. "Don't call me Master," she demanded in a master-like tone, "or I'll beat you up!" I complied, but only in order to avoid getting beat up, which, as you might imagine, made me feel like a slave.

Did the experiment yield the info I was looking for? Yes, but only because she knew I wasn't serious, so we could laugh it off. To my satisfaction, it did prove my hunch true. I am absolutely certain that people who are in love should not relate to one another as masters and slaves.

Why not?

Well, for one thing, you might get beat up. But more importantly, you could never bring satisfaction to the one who loves you by relating to them as a slave. To do so would suggest that the relationship is not founded on love.

When the day's experiment was over, I eagerly shifted back to the husband-wife way of relating. Could it be that God wants all of us to make just such a shift in our relationship with Him?

No *could be* about it. Scripture is clear. God is deeply longing for a radical change in our perception of Him and our way of relating to Him. Listen as He speaks His earnest hope:

She "'went after her lovers;

But Me she forgot,' says the Lord.

'Therefore, behold, I will allure her,
Will bring her into the wilderness,
And speak comfort to her . . .
And it shall be, in that day,'
Says the Lord,
'That you will call Me 'My Husband,'
And no longer call Me 'My Master'" (Hosea 2:13-17).

Try to comprehend what God is saying to us in this extremely meaningful passage. Here is presented a sharp contrast between two very distinct pictures of God, and two very distinct ways of relating to Him. One is true and the other is a false conception we have received as a legacy from the fall of our first parents, Adam and Eve. As we noted in a previous chapter, Satan led the Eden couple into sin by misrepresenting God's character. Three key features composed the deception:

1. God has arbitrarily and unnecessarily restricted your freedom to keep you in bondage (Genesis 3:1).

2. Therefore, He has lied to you about the effect of asserting your liberty, claiming you will die when, in fact, you will not (Genesis 3:4).

3. The reason He has restricted you in this dominating manner and lied to you is to keep you from becoming equal with Him. God is essentially self-centered and does not have your best interest at heart (Genesis 3:5).

Such was the distorted picture painted on the inner canvas of the human heart by the fallen angel, a portrait that made God out to be an arbitrary, restrictive, self-centered slave-master. By venturing into sin, Adam and Eve believed God to be the kind of person suggested by the Deceiver. It is evident, therefore, that the slavemaster picture of God lay at the foundation of the sin problem.

Once the false image was embraced, the situation became even more complicated. The severe sense of guilt that rightfully attended Adam and Eve's transgression served to reinforce the lie now residing in their darkened perception. When feelings of condemnation flooded into their minds, the Nightmare Weaver was quick to further apply his dastardly art by transposing their shame over the face of God. The logical deduction of their delusion was to believe that their sense of guilt did not indicate any actual wrongdoing on their part, but was being arbitrarily imposed on them by God, their perceived enemy. On the heels of the Fall, they immediately became afraid of God.

This makes sense, because they now believed Him to be a self-serving master ruling over them as slaves.

Then came the long and sordid history of human beings attempting to appease the anger and earn the favor of a God they believed to be an arbitrary dominator. From that day of initial deception in Eden until this very moment, Satan has fine-tuned his subtle misrepresentation of God's character. Paul points out that the Adversary's chief aim is to keep our "minds . . . blinded" to the true "image of God" (2 Corinthians 4:4). Satan doesn't care if we boldly rebel against God in reaction against the false image, or if we strive to serve God as fear-motivated slaves. In either case, the true God is neither known nor worshiped.

When we come to understand that the fallen condition of mankind is based on a psychological heritage of deception regarding the character of God, we can begin to comprehend the real difference between the many false religions of the world and the one true theology. Paganism in all its forms is simply the human attempt to approach God under the influence of Satan's original misrepresentation of the divine character. Believing God to be a master ruling over humanity as slaves, men have developed various systems of worship that cannot help but reflect that misconception. God's laws are seen as arbitrary requirements He imposes on us to serve Himself, possessing no basis in a benevolent reality designed for our good. It is thought, or at least felt, that our happiness is to be found in disobedience to God's rules, for those rules restrict our pleasure and prevent our elevation. Obedience is bondage. There are no actual, inherent ill effects in sin itself, but only an unrelated punishment inflicted by God simply because His sovereign will was violated. He doesn't want us doing whatever He has forbidden, not because those actions will do us harm, but merely in order to maintain control over us.

In sharp contrast, from a biblical perspective God's law is a matter of altruistic principle rather than arbitrary requirement. Altruism is "unselfish concern for the welfare of others" (*Webster's*). In harmony with His true character, God's law is based on selfless, other-centered love (Matthew 22: 36-40; Romans 13:10). He designed all of creation for life and happiness and has, therefore, made no law that is not truly meant for our well-being and pleasure. To violate those benevolent principles brings negative consequences upon us that derive directly from sin itself. "The way of transgressors is hard"

(Proverbs 13:15, KJV). "The curse causeless shall not come" (Proverbs 26:2, KJV). "He who sins against me wrongs his own soul" (Proverbs 8:36). "And sin, when it is full-grown, brings forth death" (James 1:15).

The difference between these two pictures is dominance versus love, crystallized in Hosea as a master-slave relationship versus a husband-wife relationship.

Jesus called for the same kind of radical change in our perception of God:

"No longer do I call you servants, for a servant does not know what his Master is doing; but I have called you friends, for all things that I heard from My Father I have made known to you" (John 15:15).

This is one of the most astounding things Jesus said during His teaching ministry. Consider the implications.

First, we must realize that for Christ to say such a thing clearly indicates that His followers were, in fact, viewing their relationship with God as a master-servant arrangement. No one says, "Stop bouncing that ball off the wall," unless, of course, a ball is being bounced off the wall. The fact that Jesus said, "I do not want you to relate to Me as servants to a master," means they were doing just that, even as we do today.

Second, we must ask the logical question, "What could possibly be wrong with relating to the Monarch of the universe as servants in subjection to a master?" After all, He is the almighty Creator, and we are rebels spared by His sheer mercy. Should we not get on our faces and tremble in fear awaiting His demands?

Yes, the fact that we are sinners rightfully drives us to that humble position. But the astounding truth is that He refuses to accept that kind of arrangement, when He would certainly be justified in doing so. Like the prodigal son, we say, "I am no longer worthy to be called your son. Make me like one of your hired servants" (Luke 15:19). No other request would be rational or real. But like the "prodigal father," apparently as "wasteful" with His love as the prodigal son was with his money, God responds by ignoring our plea for a servant's position and says, "This my son was dead and is alive again; he was lost and is found" (Luke 15:24).

In a remarkable display of mercy, God allows us to approach Him as a Master, our hearts filled with misconceptions about His character, while He endeavors to allure us into a love relationship with Himself. Jesus extended to the disciples the same compassion. He does the same for you and me. He allows us to relate to Him as a Master, all the while desiring in His heart that we would grow up in our understanding to see Him as a bridegroom and a friend. He longs to hear from our lips the Church's prophetic realization,

"Yes, He is altogether lovely.

This is my beloved,

And this is my friend" (Song of Songs 5:16).

Here is the high and beautiful end to which our spiritual experience is tending. When we finally come to see God in this light, then the long awaited announcement may be made, "Let us be glad and rejoice and give Him glory, for the marriage of the Lamb has come, and His wife has made herself ready" (Revelation 19:7).

We begin our journey as children, our hearts heavy with guilt and dark notions about God. Our spiritual life is governed by the external rule of authority. We hear God saying to us, "No! No! No!"

"Don't touch that!"

"Get that out of your mouth!"

"Thou shalt not!"

"Sit right there and don't move!"

"Why?" we ask. But we are incapable at this point of understanding the answer. So we hear Him say, "Because I said so! It is not for you to understand why, but to obey."

God looks like a master and His law feels like restrictive rules that must be kept in order to avoid punishment and to earn rewards.

"You do what I tell you, or else," we hear Him say.

"Or else what?" we ask, as slaves.

"Or else I will punish you," threatens the Master.

We grudgingly vow, "All that You say, we will do," muttering under our breath, "but we sure don't want to."

"When I was a child," says Paul of his and our spiritual growth, "I spoke as a child, I understood as a child, I thought as a child; but when I became a man, I put away childish things. For now we see in a mirror, dimly, but then face to face. Now I know in part, but then [when I grow up spiritually and put away childish thoughts] I shall know just as I also am known" (1 Corinthians 13:11-12).

God is eager for us to "grow up in all things" "to the measure of the stature of the fullness of Christ" (Ephesians 4:15, 13). There comes a time in every spiritual journey when one must put away childish thoughts and understandings about God. We either continue to serve God as slaves and become spiritually retarded or we mature to love Him as His faithful bride. Ezekiel 16:8 calls this juncture "the time . . . for you to fall in love" (TEV). This is when we move from being governed by the external rule of authority to the internal rule of love.

When we understand that God created us with free hearts designed for love, not as robots designed to perform mechanical functions, or as slaves to render Him obligatory service, the divine-human romance passages of Scripture will make perfect sense. They tell us a part of God's story that will bring tears to our eyes. If we continue attempting to serve God with a slave-master mentality, moved merely by fear of being lost and desire for the rewards of Heaven, we will find the love-relationship language of the Bible to be foreign, mysterious, perhaps even offensive. No tears will form in our eyes, for there is no heart as of yet to our religion, and tears only flow from the heart.

Hosea's prophecy clearly calls for a revolutionary paradigm shift in our perception of God and our manner of relating to Him. The Creator looks forward to "that day" when His people, you and me included, will "no longer" call Him "Master," but rather "Husband." The most radical thing you will ever do is allow your heart to see God as He really is, contrary to what you have received as a legacy from the Fall, contrary to what you have been taught and contrary to what you have believed the Bible was saying to you when you read it with the understanding of a child. This amazing refashioning of our relationship with God can only take place as we deeply internalize His love as it was revealed in Christ. The alluring demonstration of God's love at the cross (1) tells the truth about God's character in contrast to Satan's lie, (2) convinces us that God is not standing toward us with condemnation, but rather with mercy, (3) casts out our slavish fear of God as a dominating Master, and (4) makes it possible for us to see and relate to Him as to a loving Husband.

—*Chapter Fifteen*—

A Heart That Can See, Feel and Move
COVENANTS

There is a heart afraid to see . . .
 Shall vision of Him also reveal me?
There is a heart afraid to feel . . .
 Will love's emotion my hatred steal?
There is a heart afraid to move . . .
 If self I abandon, will self I lose?

GOD IS ON bended knee before you. His arms are outstretched, right palm open to invite movement toward Him, left hand tightly clinched with hopeful passion. He forthrightly declares His heart's desire:

"I will make you My promised bride forever.

I will be good and fair;

I will show you My love and mercy.

I will be true to you as My promised bride,

And you will know the Lord" (Hosea 2:19-20, NCV).

What is your answer to His proposal? If yes, then you have chosen to make the Master-to-Husband paradigm shift explored in the previous chapter. You are moving into what the Bible calls the "new covenant," also referred to as a "marriage covenant."

"As I passed by again, I saw that the time had come for you to fall in love. I covered your naked body with my coat and promised to love you. Yes, I made a marriage covenant with you, and you became Mine.' This is what the Sovereign Lord says" (Ezekiel 16:8, TEV).

Clearly, this is a covenant of love, for in it God has "promised to love" us and He is hopeful that we will "fall in love" with Him in response. God's promise of love is the firm foundation on which the covenant is based. Our love for Him is a responsive reflection of His love. Hence, even our love is His achievement, not ours. And therein lies the secret power of the new covenant.

Under the overarching promise of God's love, there are three main elements that together compose the new covenant:

1. The promise of restored vision.

2. The promise of restored sensitivity.

3. The promise of restored moral power.

Allow me to give you a brief tour of this rich topic.

The Promise of Restored Vision

As we have noted previously, the most foundational level on which sin has impacted us is in our ability to see God as He is. By means of deception and guilt Satan has succeeded in distorting our perceptual vision of God's character. Whereas before the Fall, the human heart knew God to be a kind Father and a loving Friend, after sin entered upon the scene our sight was blinded by lies and we became afraid of Him.

The new covenant promises that our knowledge of God's true character will be restored:

"For this is the covenant . . . None of them shall teach his neighbor, and none his brother, saying, 'Know the Lord,' for all shall know Me, from the least of them to the greatest of them. For I will be merciful to their unrighteousness, and their sins and their lawless deeds I will remember no more" (Hebrews 8:10-12).

As I have pointed out previously in this book, the word "know" refers to intimate, firsthand experience in God's love. It is the purpose of God in the new covenant that each one of us would know Him in this way, with such clarity that it would become unnecessary to admonish one another, saying, "Know the Lord."

However, leading up to this point of common intimacy with God, and for its ultimate achievement, we must realize that our entire witness to the world and all preaching to the church is for the single purpose of saying to one and all, "Know the Lord." The crucial objective of the gospel is to magnify the beauty of God's character so that all may truly come to know Him, *personally* know Him, as the new covenant anticipates. If we think God has called us to fill the church pews with as many people as possible, as fast as possible, with a low-grade intellectual knowledge of doctrinal facts, we are only complicating the gospel commission rather than fulfilling it. The prophet Isaiah clearly tells us what the content of the gospel proclamation should be:

"You who bring good tidings [the gospel],

Lift up your voice with strength,

Lift it up, be not afraid;

Say to the cities of Judah,

'Behold your God!'" (Isaiah 40:9).

The gospel is *about* God. It is not *about* any particular set of doctrines or prophecies or lifestyle standards, except as those things are communicated in such a way as to contribute to the vital message at hand, "Behold your God!" The truth of His righteous, trustworthy character is the good news the world needs, in contrast to the lies Satan has woven and spun to hide God from view.

Paul concurs with Isaiah:

"The gospel of Christ . . . is the power of God to salvation for everyone who believes . . . for in it the righteousness of God is revealed from faith to faith" (Romans 1:16-17).

Catch Paul's equation here. The gospel of Christ is the power by which we are saved because it is the revelation of God's righteousness. In other words, the character of God is on display in the gospel. Therein lies its power to save.

Paul said the same thing with different words to the Corinthians. He warned that Satan is in the business of keeping minds "blinded" to "the light of the gospel of the glory of Christ, who is the image of God . . . For it is God who commanded light to shine out of darkness, who has shone in our hearts to give the light of the knowledge of the glory of God in the face of Jesus Christ" (2 Corinthians 4:4, 6).

The equation here is the same as in Romans 1:16-17 and Isaiah 40:9. The gospel is the image of God—the glory of His character—shining bright and clear in the person of Jesus Christ.

The Promise of Restored Sensitivity

As the new covenant restores our vision of God's character, the knowledge of His love simultaneously restores to our hearts the emotional sensitivity with which we were originally created. Not only has sin blurred our perception of God's character, but it has also blunted our ability to feel God's feelings and the feelings of others with sympathetic vibration. According to Jesus, "blinded . . . eyes [minds]" and "hardened . . . hearts" go together (John 12:40). Paul teaches us that our hearts are "hardened through the deceitfulness of sin" (Hebrews 3:13). Sin deceives us into believing God is an arbitrary, self-centered slavemaster. As the mind is blinded by this false picture, the heart becomes hard in its feelings toward God.

The new covenant promises to make our hearts soft again:

"This shall be the covenant . . . I will put My law in their inward parts, and write it in their hearts" (Jeremiah 31:33, KJV).

"I will give you a new heart and put a new spirit in you; I will remove from you your [hardened] heart of stone and give you a [sensitive] heart of flesh [that can feel]" (Ezekiel 36:26, NIV).

"I will take away your hard nature and give you a nature that can be touched" (Mof).

The longest journey you'll ever make is from your head to your heart, from mere intellectual assent to passionate emotional commitment. I say it's a long journey because sin has so hardened our finer sensibilities, and so blinded us to God's true character, that we find full-throttle devotion to Him unnatural. How do you feel, for example, when God says things to you like this:

"Yes, I have loved you with an everlasting love; therefore with lovingkindness I have drawn you" (Jeremiah 31:3).

"As I passed by again, I saw that the time had come for you to fall in love. I covered your naked body with My coat and promised to love you. Yes, I made a marriage covenant with you, and you became Mine" (Ezekiel 16:8, TEV).

Chances are, if you're like most people, you feel nothing at all when God speaks to you in this way. Most likely you don't even find it natural to personalize such words when I ask how you feel when God says these things to *you*. Our hearts are afraid to "feel after Him" (Acts 17:27, KJV). Why? Because to feel is to get real, to trust, to let go of self and become vulnerable to the pain of change and disappointment. Actually, what we're afraid of is pain, and we know that we won't feel pain if we don't feel love and trust to begin with. So we stand off at a "safe" distance from God. We make religious claims. We go through religious forms and ceremonies. We engage in religious discussions. But we are reluctant to love God with all our heart, soul, mind and strength (Mark 12:30).

To *think* about God is vital. But to think thoughts about God that keep us from *feeling* for Him is a cunning way of forgetting God under the pretense of remembering Him. All true obedience comes from the heart. All genuine spiritual experience awakens a rich current of deep and sacred emotions toward God. Mental assent to doctrinal facts about God does not constitute real commitment to Him. And yet, what we think and believe about God is vital, because thought is the foundation of feeling. We cannot feel right and true feelings toward God until we first think right and true thoughts about God. We need to see Him as He is with the intellect in order to feel Him as He is with the emotions. The highest and clearest thoughts about God give birth to the deepest and truest feelings for Him. There is such a thing as empty emotion without true meaning, but there is no such thing as true meaning without emotion. In learning and believing the truth about God, we will come to love Him with all the energy we possess.

To know God is not merely an intellectual endeavor, as if He could be ascertained by simply collecting and memorizing bare facts about Him. Rather, to really know God is to both see with the mind and feel with the heart. To know God is to love Him—with "all your heart, with all your soul, and with all your mind" (Matthew 22:37). To quote Paul, the love of God "passes knowledge" (Ephesians 3:19). It soars high above intellectual pursuit alone. If God's love is to be known, it must be experienced. It must be allowed access to the emotions as well as to the intellect.

The Promise of Restored Moral Power

As the new covenant restores clear understanding of God's character to our minds, and restores to our hearts a revived emotional sensitivity that makes us responsive to His overtures, there arises within us a powerful new motivation to do always and only those things that please Him. Because it is a covenant of love, it is also a covenant of power.

"This is the covenant that I will make with them after those days, says the Lord: I will put My laws into their hearts, and in their minds I will write them" (Hebrews 10:16).

"I will give you a new heart and put a new spirit within you; I will take the heart of stone out of your flesh and give you a heart of flesh. I will put My Spirit within you and cause you to walk in My statutes, and you will keep My judgments and do them" (Ezekiel 36:26-27).

The all-elusive obedience to God's law, which we have found so impossible to achieve, becomes a reality in the new covenant. When God gets into our hearts and minds by the revelation of His love, He is within us a causal power by which we are enabled to "walk in," "keep," and "do" His law. As the apostle Paul says, when we "comprehend" and "know the love of Christ," it becomes an aggressive "power that works in us" (Ephesians 3:18-20).

Paul suggests in the seventh chapter of Romans that the old covenant is like being married to the law as an impersonal list of rules, while not knowing the love of Christ as our Savior-Husband. In the old covenant paradigm we are alive to the law's requirements, its forbiddings and its condemnation for our failures to obey, but we are oblivious to the personal heart of God toward us. We see the law's demands and our sins against which it stands, but we don't see God's merciful love. All we can do in this bleak framework of understanding is "serve . . . in the oldness of the letter" (7:6); that is, we attempt to obey the outward letter of the law, rendering slavelike service to God out of a sense of heartless obligation.

The new covenant, on the other hand, is marriage to Christ. We yield our hearts to Him in the alluring light of His self-sacrificing love made clear at Calvary. With the cross in full view we "become dead to the law through the body of Christ, that [we] may be married to another—to Him who was raised from the dead, that we should bear fruit to God" (Romans 7:4). In the new covenant paradigm our hearts are alive to God's forgiving mercy and dead to the law's condemnation. Rather than attempting to keep the letter of the law as a means of salvation, we "serve in the newness of spirit and not in the oldness of the letter" (verse 6). Love, not condemnation, is the motive for obedience.

In 2 Corinthians 3 Paul draws the same contrast between the old and new covenants, but with added insight. He begins with the straightforward statement, we are "ministers of the new covenant, not of the letter but of the Spirit; for the letter kills, but the Spirit gives life" (verse 6). Then he explains why and how the letter of the law kills. It is a "ministry of death, written and engraved on stones" (verse 7). Then he calls it "the ministry of condemnation" (verse 9). In other words, the letter of the law written on stone only has power to impose condemnation and, by its condemnation, to judge us worthy of death. The law of itself possesses absolutely no saving power, and all attempts to keep the law as a means of salvation only serve to accentuate our guilt.

In contrast, Paul explains that the new covenant "gives life" rather than death because it is a "ministry of righteousness" rather than "condemnation." That is to say, Christ administers to us the free gift of His righteousness, through which we stand forgiven before God. "The veil [of darkness and separation from God] is taken away in Christ" (verse 14). All that has obstructed our vision of God—namely, our sin and its attending guilt—is removed as we see His merciful love in the life and death of Jesus.

Paul then makes a summarizing statement about how the new covenant works to change our lives:

"We all, with unveiled face, beholding as in a mirror the glory of the Lord, are being transformed into the same image from glory to glory, just as by the Spirit of the Lord" (2 Corinthians 3:18).

What an incredible promise!

It is quite clear that the secret power of the new covenant, to accomplish all that the old covenant could not, is in directing our focus out of ourselves to behold the glory of God's character in Christ. The new covenant calls us to *look at someone*, not to *do something;* and in looking, to believe the promises God has fulfilled in Christ rather than make promises we are powerless to keep. And then, as we behold and believe all that God has done for us in the Savior, the needed changes in our lives that we could never achieve in old heart will be achieved "by the Spirit of the Lord" in the new heart God has created within us by His love.

A heart that can *see* the true beauty of His character.

A heart that can *feel* emotionally responsive to His love.

And a heart that can *move* in free obedience to His holy law.

— *Chapter Sixteen* —

Penetrating the Veil
MEDITATION

"See, He is on the other
    Side of our wall,
He is looking in at the windows,
    Letting Himself be seen
Through the spaces."
    Song of Solomon 2:9, B.A.S.

Gᴏᴅ ɪꜱ ɪɴ a fragile and painful predicament. He yearns to be close to us, but He must keep a safe distance for our sakes. He wants us to know Him just as He is, but we can't bear the whole truth all at once. His heart beats with urgent longing to fully disclose His love, but we would disintegrate in shame for what we would see in ourselves by contrast. The very thing He desires most to give us would be our complete undoing.

To Moses God said, "You cannot see My face; for no man shall see Me, and live" (Exodus 33:20).

Isaiah received a glimpse of "the Lord sitting on a throne, high and lifted up," surrounded with "smoke" to make the vision bearable. Even so, the prophet's consciousness was flooded with realizations of his own sinfulness, and he cried out, "Woe is me, for I am undone" (Isaiah 6:1, 4-5). "Oh, no! I will be destroyed" (NCV). "I am lost" (NEB). "I am ruined!" (NIV).

When Daniel saw a vision of the pre-incarnate Christ, he said, "My comeliness [beauty] was turned in me into corruption" (Daniel 10:8, KJV).

These Scriptures do not intend to communicate capricious hostility on God's part. The reason we cannot survive in His presence is not because He will not tolerate *us*, but because He cannot tolerate *our sin*. Therefore, we cannot tolerate Him. That is to say, we cannot bear to encounter the full reality of His holy, selfless, sinless love because it would ignite within us a perfect consciousness of our sinfulness by contrast and the guilt would destroy us.

A fragile and painful predicament, indeed!

So what is the Lover of our souls to do when His very love is lethal to our souls, and yet we will just as surely perish without it?

He must allow Himself to be hidden.

Not in order to *evade* us, but in order to *invade* us in such a way as to preserve our lives while establishing the contact vital to our salvation; in order, as well, that He will one day be able to commune with us face to face. God's mercy affords Him no other choice than to recede behind the veil of His heavenly temple as we hide behind the veil of our distorted perceptions. Our "veil," says Paul, is our blindness of "mind" and "heart" through which we cannot penetrate to behold His glory (2 Corinthians 3:14-18). To us, for us, He has become "the Presence behind the veil" (Hebrews 6:19), bearing the blame and reproach of the dark rumors we have believed about Him. Love "bears all things" (1 Corinthians 13:7).

"He is on the other side of our wall," behind the barrier of self-justification and blame we have erected to evade our guilt. "Adam and his wife hid themselves from the presence of the Lord God" (Genesis 3:8), and we still hide. Says the prophet, "Your iniquities have separated you from your God; and your sins have hidden His face from you" (Isaiah 59:2). And yet, from "the other side of our wall, He is looking in at the windows" of our understanding, "letting Himself be seen through the spaces," eagerly striving to communicate His innocent love in every way possible without violating our freedom or overwhelming our hearts.

What tender and merciful love!

The divine-human person of Jesus Christ is God's gentle penetration through the veil into our benighted presence. To "sweep away the refuge of lies" in which we trust and "overflow the hiding place" in which we hide is the reason He came to our world (Isaiah 28:17). Announcing His point of origin and the nature of His mission, He said, "No one has seen God at any time. The only begotten Son, who is in the bosom of the Father, He has declared Him" (John 1:18). "This one-of-a-kind God-Expression, who exists at the very heart of the Father, has made Him plain as day" (TM). Summarizing the circle He traversed for our salvation, Jesus said, "I came out from the Father and have come into the world; again, I am leaving the world and going to the Father" (John 16:28, AB). He came out from "the Presence behind the veil" (Hebrews 6:19), "made Him plain as day," and then went back bearing our humanity. As a snapshot, this is the basic picture of what Jesus did to save us. Out and down He came; up and in He returned. Hold that image in your heart, let it incubate for the rest of your life, and all that is dark about God will vanish away like mist before the rising sun.

As in Christ God has penetrated the veil to where we are, so also in Christ we may now penetrate through the veil to where He is:

"Therefore, brethren, having boldness to enter the Holiest by the blood of Jesus, by a new and living way which He consecrated for us, through the veil, that is, His flesh, and having a High Priest over the house of God, let us draw near with a true heart in full assurance of faith, having our hearts sprinkled from an evil conscience and our bodies washed with pure water" (Hebrews 10:19-22).

"This hope we have as an anchor of the soul, both sure and steadfast, and which enters the Presence behind the veil, where the Forerunner has entered for us, even Jesus, having become High Priest forever" (Hebrews 6:19-20).

Jesus came out from the Father, took hold of us by the heart, and now as our High Priestly Mediator He escorts us back to "the Presence behind the veil." By virtue of His shed blood as a sacrifice of selfless love, we may have "boldness to enter the Holiest" place in all the universe—the inner chamber of the sanctuary where the Father eagerly awaits our coming. We are privileged to "draw near with a true heart in full assurance of faith," absolutely certain that what Jesus has revealed about the Father is indeed true. With no fear of rejection, filled with complete confidence that we are loved and accepted, we may follow our "Forerunner" into the Father's presence.

The Greek word here translated "Forerunner" literally means "scout." A scout is one who goes ahead of others to investigate conditions of terrain and whether there are hostile or friendly persons ahead. This word picture of our Mediator indicates that He knows the Presence behind the veil is friendly. We can proceed forward with bold assurance and confidence, following our Scout behind the veil. Jesus has not penetrated the veil *for* us, *instead* of us; rather, He has gone there *as* us, *before* us, desiring that we would believe His good report about the Father and follow His lead. He has forged a path of truth through the darkness into the perfect light of the Father's love.

Mediation is a subject often infused with distorted ideas about God. We humans tend to see what we believe, rather than believe what we see. Like Charisa in chapter nine, who saw evil in the king's countenance because she believed the dark rumor before ever meeting him, we are inclined to interpret Bible doctrines according to the dark fears we harbor about God. We take a truth like *Divine Omnipotence* and come up with a predestination doctrine that removes all real human freedom and makes God look like an insecure control freak. In doing so, we have turned *Substitutionary Atonement* into a third-party-appeasement concept that makes God appear vindictive and arbitrary. (See my book, *Shades of Grace*, for a more detailed treatment of this subject.) We tweak the doctrine of *Obedience* into a fear-motivated obligation, *Grace* into an abolition of law, and *Heaven* into a divine bribe. The common denominator in all false doctrine is that God looks bad and we look either good or victimized.

The Bible truth of *Mediation* is no exception, not having been spared the darkness that projects out of us onto all we see. We imagine that our need for a mediator between God and us means there is some difference in character between Jesus and the Father. The idea is that the loving, merciful Jesus pleads with the just and wrathful Father to refrain from doing us the harm He would like to. Justice in this paradigm is thought to be, or at least felt to be, arbitrary punishment. The cross is viewed as God satiating His anger by inflicting pain and death on Jesus, our Substitute. Then, as our Mediator, Jesus acts as a shield to block God's anger from reaching us by continually reminding the Father that He bore it for us.

Father	Jesus	Sinner
○——— Justice ———⊛	——— Mercy ———⊛	

There are elements of truth in this picture, but it is mixed with just enough falsehood and imbalanced emphasis to misrepresent the character of God. The Bible teaches something significantly different about mediation. First, it must be understood that the Father and the Son are one in character and purpose. This is the vital foundational truth that must be realized in order to comprehend the true meaning of mediation. Both God the Father and God the Son are holy, righteous and just. Both hate sin with a perfect hatred and can never be reconciled to it. There is no difference between them in this respect. Both are also merciful, kind and forgiving. No difference here either. In relation to sinners, in both the heart of the Father and the heart of the Son, "mercy triumphs over judgment" (James 2:13). In other words, while they both discern and abhor our sin with an immutable justice, "where sin abounded, grace abounded much more" (Romans 5:20). There is absolutely no dichotomy of character between the Father and the Son. If the Father had come into our world as the incarnate One rather than the Son, there would have been no difference at all in what we would have seen. "He who has seen Me has seen the Father," Jesus declared (John 14:9).

So, then, why is there a need for mediation and what purpose does such an arrangement serve? The answer is very encouraging.

The *justice* dimension of God's character is not at all arbitrary. The word simply refers to that which is *true* and *right*. When wrong is done, justice takes on the form of a very real and intrinsic condemnation of sin that unavoidably occurs in the light of God's absolute perfection and His righteous hatred of sin. Because of what sin is, we sinners cannot endure unveiled encounter with God, for in His presence all things are "exposed" (Ephesians 5:13), "naked and open" (Hebrews 4:13). Conscience would be made alive and acute in its awareness of our sin and the guilt would crush us as it did Jesus at the cross. The only reason we could encounter Christ and not die was because His divinity was shrouded in our humanity. Even so, we could not endure Him for long. We crucified the Light of Life because His love confronted us with our sinfulness. Jesus pointed out this tension when He said, "You seek to kill Me, a Man who has told you the truth" (John 8:40).

The *mercy* dimension of God's character is His spontaneous response of compassion toward wrongdoers. God knows no mercy for *sin* itself. It is completely contrary to all He is. It is diametrically opposed to His love. But for the *sinner*, the *person* whom God loves more than His own life, there is abundant mercy. Mercy is the forgiveness of a personal God for persons who have sinned. The *sinner* can be saved; *sin* cannot, for it cannot exist in God's presence. The plan of salvation intends to destroy sin while preserving the sinner, making it possible for humanity to once more enjoy face-to-face friendship with God. Mediation is the means by which this delicate purpose is to be achieved.

When poor Job was suffering confusion about God's character, his only enlightened friend, Elihu, explained his need for a mediator:

"If there is a messenger for him [man],
A mediator, one among a thousand,
To show man His [God's] uprightness,
Then He [God] is [seen to be] gracious to him [man], and says,
'Deliver him from going down to the Pit;
I have found a ransom . . .
He shall pray to God, and He will delight in him,
He [man] will see His [God's] face with joy,
For He restores to man [knowledge of] His righteousness.

Then he looks at men and says,

'I have sinned, and perverted what was right,

And it did not profit me.'

He [God] will redeem his soul from going down to the Pit,

And his life shall see the light . . . that he may be enlightened with the light of life" (Job 33:23-30).

This is the earliest biblical articulation of mediation and perhaps the clearest. In a prophetic sense it points to the Messiah who was yet to come as the Substitute and Mediator of the human race. Notice that the "Mediator" is a "Messenger" who fulfills the purpose of mediation by showing man two truths about God: His "uprightness" and the fact that He is "gracious." By the word "uprightness" is meant "justice." By the word "gracious" is meant "mercy." The Mediator will not lay aside justice for mercy, nor will He lay aside mercy for justice. He will maintain God's justice while revealing His mercy. In keeping with the idea that the Mediator is a revealer of the truth about God, the King James Version uses the word "Interpreter" instead of "Mediator" in this passage. The Mediator is one who interprets God's character to the dim perception of man, leading him to "see" God's true "face with joy."

Also notice that in the Mediator God has found a "ransom." This is an early reference to the concept of substitution. The Hebrew word here translated "ransom" means to "cover," "bear" or "carry," from which we derive the idea of *payment,* as in, "I will *cover* the cost of your dinner," or "I will *bear* the expense of your debt." The Mediator interprets or communicates God's righteousness and grace by bearing our sins with forgiveness and by covering the cost of our transgressions with His own suffering.

The mediation of Jesus is not a *shield* from God's wrath, but rather a *channel* through which the full reality of His holy love may be revealed to us in healing doses. What we see in the Mediator is the truth about the Father.

Father   Jesus   Sinner

Jesus explained that His mediatory role is a temporary arrangement that will one day cease as we come to know the Father's love:

"I have spoken to you in figurative language; but the time is coming when I will no longer speak to you in figurative language, but I will tell you plainly about the Father. In that day you will ask in My name, and I do not say to you that I shall pray the Father for you; for the Father Himself loves you" (John 16:25-27).

This is a truly amazing statement our Savior has made to us. Unpack it with me point by point.

First notice that Jesus tells us that His teaching ministry was "*about* the Father." The grand central theme of all He lived and taught was the character of God.

More specifically, He wants each individual to know and believe that "the Father Himself loves you." This is the vital, life-giving reality we don't see. Even when we give mental assent to God's love, we often don't really know and believe it in our inmost heart. With our mouth we may say, "God is love," because we know this is what we ought to say. But on a personal level, emotionally and behaviorally, we do not feel or act as though the Father loves us. The presence of sin and guilt in our lives belies our intellectual profession. We may speak of God's love as a fact and yet not feel it as a transforming truth.

Jesus emphasized that "the Father *Himself* loves you." We are inclined to believe that Jesus loves us, but are not as sure that the Father Himself loves us just the same. As our Mediator, Jesus the Man has taken the world in His tender human arms. And then, as we cease to tremble and begin to rest in His embrace, He whispers, "I'm God."

"You are God?!" we respond in astonishment. "You are the One from whom we have fled in fear? Surely we have believed lies about You, for now we see merciful love where once we saw only condemnation and wrath."

All the love we see and feel radiating from Jesus is the very love of the Father. And yet Jesus found it necessary to teach us about the Father with "figurative language." Earlier He had told the disciples, "I still have many things to say to you, but you cannot bear them now" (John 16:12). The next verse makes it clear that what we cannot "bear" is "all truth" (verse 13). While God is not the author of the lies about Himself that enshroud our minds, He must lead us out of the darkness carefully, by degrees, as we can "bear" the splendor of His light. To be immediately confronted with "all truth" would be more than we could endure, so He allows us to approach Him with varying degrees of self-preserving darkness upon our perception.

As the one true Iconoclast He accepts us while we still believe falsehoods about Him, eager to destroy all false images and lead us into perfect vision of Himself as fast as we can assimilate it. What we regard as ultimate truth may, in fact, be a gray mixture of light and darkness in need of purification. Mediation is God's merciful, condescending way of relating to us while we are in darkness in order to convey the whole truth about Himself. As the "one Mediator between God and man" (1 Timothy 2:5), Jesus serves to subdue the radiant splendor of God's glory to a bearable level, opening to us a way by which we may come into vital communion with God and live. Once communication is established, a process of progressive enlightenment begins to transpire, escorting us step by step into the full knowledge of God's holy love.

While Jesus communicated with "figurative language," He looked forward to "the time" when He could tell us "plainly about the Father." All His parables are veiled revelations of the character of God. Each symbolic tale He told was intended to communicate, either by comparison or by contrast, the truth of God's perfect love. His repeated opening line—"the kingdom of heaven is like unto"—points to a King who governs His domain in the just and merciful ways highlighted in the stories. Each parable says something about the character of God our King.

The same is true of Scripture as a whole. When all figurative language is decoded, all symbols traced to their substance, all parables unraveled to their ultimate point, all shadows consumed by perfect light—there is seen to be one hidden truth laced like threads of gold throughout the Bible: "The Father Himself loves you." The symbolic sanctuary service of the Old Testament only served to foreshadow the ultimate antitypical reality of final and full atonement, perfect oneness with the "Presence behind the veil" in the Most Holy place. The biblical narratives of God's interactions with men and women are but turnings of the diamond of God's multifaceted character in order to compose a picture of what kind of person He is. Even the Ten Commandment Law, while a definite high point of divine revelation, "had no glory in this respect, because of the glory that excels" (2 Corinthians 3:10). It was a lesser glory in comparison to "the surpassing glory" (NIV) of God's love manifested in Christ. The law was "written and engraved on stones" as a transcript of God's character (2 Corinthians 3:7). But in Jesus the Father's character was personified as a living reality.

When we finally know and believe that the Father Himself loves us with the very same love we see in Jesus, then mediation will no longer be necessary. "In that day," Christ explained, "you will ask in My name [approach the Father through Me as a mediator], and I do not say to you that I shall pray the Father for you; for the Father Himself loves you." Jesus wants us to understand that His role as our Mediator in no way implies a lack of love on the Father's part. His mediation only serves to take us by the hand and lead us to the Father, to "the Presence behind the veil." It is a temporary intervention to meet us in our fallen state—a lens, a window, even a magnifying glass into the Father's heart. The whole point of the plan of salvation is to usher us into a completely restored, face-to-face fellowship with the Father with no wall between.

I know you long for that day, as do I.

Then let us follow our Forerunner where He leads.

"Come on," He says, "it is OK. The Father is good and kind. He loves you, just as I do. Yes, He is infinitely just, but He has forgiven all your sins. Follow Me into His presence. You don't have to be afraid."

— Chapter Seventeen —

How Invasive, This Love
JUDGMENT

Firelight shining deep,
  Revealing what I hide inside;
Consume the lies that in me creep,
  Flames to wash me as I'm tried.

D<small>O YOU KNOW</small> yourself? I mean truly know yourself, just as you are?

Me neither.

Would you like to?

Me neither.

But, fact is, there's no way around it—that is, if we want to know God just as He is. It is absolutely unavoidable that coming to know God involves a corresponding growth in self-awareness. These two perceptual experiences occur in our hearts together, or not at all. "God is light" (1 John 1:5), and it is the nature of light to illuminate. Light increases visibility. When it shines, we see things that were before hidden by darkness. Light is an agent of exposure. As Paul says, "All things that are exposed are made manifest by the light" (Ephesians 5:13).

Scripture views our entire spiritual life as a journey of enlightenment:

"The path of the just is like the shining sun, that shines ever brighter unto the perfect day" (Proverbs 4:18).

In this verse we have a key to understanding what God intends for us as we find our way back to life in His love. The word "path" communicates the idea of a journey, which implies movement toward a specific destination. Of course this journey is not taken on a literal footpath; rather, it is a spiritual quest that entails movement in our thoughts and feelings and behavior.

What kind of movement?

Movement "like the shining sun, that shines ever brighter unto the perfect day." Movement into brighter and brighter light, and hence clearer and clearer vision, until "perfect" clarity is achieved. Unraveling the symbolism of this tightly packed Scripture, we might paraphrase it something like this:

"The life journey of the one who is going the right way is an experience of gradually increasing enlightenment, clearer perception leading to clearer perception, climaxing with perfect light."

The next logical point of interest is to ascertain the *subject* of this enlightenment process. What is the light about? What exactly do we need to see that is hidden by darkness?

We find the answer in 2 Corinthians 3:18:

"We all, with unveiled face, beholding as in a mirror the glory of the Lord, are being transformed into the same image from glory to glory, just as by the Spirit of the Lord."

Notice the striking conceptual resemblance to Proverbs 4:18. Whereas Solomon presents before us a journey of enlightenment on a path, Paul speaks of beholding God's glory in a mirror. At first glance this seems like a strange thing to say, because a mirror is generally used for seeing one's self, not for beholding someone else. Was Paul confused or just sloppy in his use of symbolism? Far from it. Actually, the apparent oddity is an ingenious insight. By using the metaphor of a mirror, Paul has told us that the very act of beholding God is itself like looking into a mirror. When we behold God, we are exposed to the illuminating light of perfect love and holiness. That light reacts in our minds like a mirror, showing us ourselves by contrast. Those who focus on themselves—their successes and failures—never really see themselves as they are. Only as we look away from ourselves to God do we begin to see ourselves clearly.

Allow me to illustrate how this works.

Go alone to a room with a mirror. Stand before the mirror and make direct eye contact with yourself. Don't laugh. Don't even crack a smile. Put on your dead-serious look, the one you get when you tell the kids you're not going to tell them again . . . for the third time. I said don't smile. Just look. Look at you.

What do you see?

If all you see is a great looking Homo sapien, you're blind. Keep looking. If all you see are lips and eyes and the need for a haircut, you still don't see the person you really are. Keep looking. Look at the person you are. Try to see what is truly there, behind your eyes. See history—hours, days, weeks, years. See deeds done and deeds left undone. See a conscious, freewill person unlike any other, formed by choices, molded by the passage of time, shaped by the thoughts and feelings and actions that have filled your time.

Who is that person in the mirror?

At least you are beginning to see an individual whose identity is defined by character, not by physical features. And yet, you still do not see yourself as you are. There are shadows cast over the person in that mirror. There are lies you have told yourself, subtle spins you have crafted to hide from yourself. "The heart is deceitful above all things, and desperately wicked; who can know it?" (Jeremiah 17:9). You have told yourself the story of your life the way you would like it to be, with just enough admission of wrong to give the appearance of honesty, but not enough to actually be honest. Like all of us, you are a "dream weaver." As such, you don't really see yourself just as you are. Welcome to the costume party!

Now here's the odd twist of truth, and yet it's not so odd when you stop and think about it: no matter how long and hard you look, you will never see yourself by looking at yourself.

But now try something different. As you stand there before the mirror, eye to eye with yourself, relax your gaze and shift it slightly to one side, off of yourself and onto God. Fasten your focus on every feature and contour of His character revealed in the "face of Jesus Christ" (2 Corinthians 4:6). As you behold Him, you will see virtue and beauty and selfless love and holiness and kindness and . . . and . . . and everything that composes utter perfection. Allow your eyes to shift back to yourself ever so briefly, then quickly back to Him. To yourself, then to Him. To yourself, to Him. His character is the truer mirror, is it not? Gradually, as you see Him more and more clearly, you will see yourself as you truly are. You will see deep need and absolute helplessness. You will see lies you have told yourself and others. You will see jealousy, envy, lust, even hate. You will see ghastly selfishness that will take your breath away with shame. The contrast between Him and you will be painful at times, but not unbearable if you keep focused on Him.

Here's the amazing thing about living your life in front of the mirror of God's character. All you have to do is keep saying *yes* to what you see in Him and *no* to what you see in yourself, and gradually the two images will merge. Contrast will lessen and harmony will increase, until at last, "when He shall appear, we shall be like Him, for we shall see Him as He is" (1 John 3:2, KJV). You will undergo a steady process of transformation into His likeness. The pain of shame will give way to the pleasure of being loved by Him and loving Him in return.

Paul uses the mirror metaphor again in 1 Corinthians 13. First he describes the selfless nature of genuine love:

"Love suffers long and is kind; love does not envy; love does not parade itself, is not puffed up; does not behave rudely, does not seek its own, is not provoked, thinks no evil; does not rejoice in iniquity, but rejoices in the truth; bears all things, believes all things, hopes all things, endures all things. Love never fails" (verses 4-8).

Then the apostle explains that God is leading us into perfect harmony with His love as we stand before the mirror of His character. Read Paul's words carefully:

"For we know in part, and we prophesy in part. But when that which is perfect has come, then that which is in part will be done away. When I was a child, I spoke as a child, I understood as a child, I thought as a child; but when I became a man, I put away childish things. For now we see in a mirror, dimly, but then face to face. Now I know in part, but then I shall know just as I also am known" (verses 9-13).

What is it that we know only in part? The context would suggest that Paul is referring to God's love, and hence to God Himself. But we are headed for "perfect" clarity, according to the apostle. "Dim" vision of God's character will be "done away" with as we remain before the mirror. When Paul says we will eventually find ourselves "face to face," and that we will "know just as [we] also [are] known," he does not implicitly state with whom we will be face to face, and who we will know just as we are known. The mirror implies that he has both God and ourselves in mind. We will be brought to the place where we are "face to face" with God and with ourselves.

James affirms that our interpretation of the mirror symbolism is accurate. He likens God's "word" and His "perfect law" to a "mirror" in which a person "observes himself" and learns "what kind of man he" is (James 1:23-25). Of God's law, Scripture says: "By the law is the knowledge of sin" (Romans 3:20). "For the commandment is a lamp, and the law a light" (Proverbs 6:23). Said another way, to see the light of God's law is to also see our sin by contrast.

Of God's word, we read: "The word of God is living and powerful, and sharper than any two-edged sword, piercing even to the division of soul and spirit, and of joints and marrow, and is a discerner of the thoughts and intents of the heart. And there is no creature hidden from His sight, but all things are naked and open to the eyes of Him to whom we must give account" (Hebrews 4:12-13).

All serious contact with God—with His law, His word and especially with the life and death of Jesus—involves conflict with self. The nature of that conflict is that we see our sin in glaring contradiction to His love and we must exercise our freedom to choose between the two. Drawing close to God always opens the heart to a sense of painful contrast while calling us in our liberty to the pleasure of greater harmony with Him. We may retain our sin and move away from God, or we may turn from our sin and move closer to Him. Every step of the way, the decision is ours.

If God is a triune fellowship of other-centered love, and if He created humanity in His image to love in freedom, and if sin is the use of our free will to live for self in rebellion against God's love, and if salvation aims to preserve the free will of sinners while drawing us back into harmony with God's love, then it should come as no surprise to us that our spiritual experience will involve a process of revelation intended to show us God's love and show us ourselves in contrast, offering us the opportunity to consciously and freely choose to accept or reject His love as the law of our lives. (Whew! That sentence is way too long. You may want to read it again.) If free will is to be preserved in the saving of our souls, then it is unavoidable that we must be led to see our sin so that we might choose to turn from it.

A preacher stood before a congregation over a century ago with this message:

"He [Jesus] gave himself for our sins; but . . . He will not take our sins—although He has bought them—without our permission. . . . Then the choice is forever with me as to whether I would rather have my sins than to have Him, isn't it? [Congregation: 'Yes.'] . . . Is that the choice before you? [Congregation: 'Yes.'] Which would you rather have, your sins or Christ? [Congregation: 'Christ.'] Then from this time henceforth can there be any hesitation about letting anything go that God shows is sin? . . . When sin is pointed out to you, say, 'I would rather have Christ than that.' And let it go. [Congregation: 'Amen.'] Just tell the Lord, 'Lord, I make the choice now; I make the trade; I make Thee my choice; it is gone, and I have something better.' Thank the Lord! Then where in the world is the opportunity for any of us to get discouraged over our sins?

"Now some of the brethren here have done that very thing. They came here free; but the Spirit of God brought up something they never saw before. The Spirit of God went deeper than it ever went before, and revealed things they never saw before; and then, instead of thanking the Lord that that was so, and letting the whole wicked business go, and thanking the Lord that they had ever so much more of Him than they ever had before, they began to get discouraged . . .

"Isn't it too bad that a person whom the Lord has loved so much as to give Himself for him at all, should act that way with the Lord, when the Lord wants to reveal more of Himself? Brethren, if any of you have got into discouragement, let us quit. If the Lord has brought up sins to us that we never thought of before, that only shows that He is going down to the depths, and He will reach the bottom at last; and when He finds the last thing that is unclean or impure, that is out of harmony with His will, and brings that up, and shows that to us, and we say, 'I would rather have the Lord than that'—then the work is complete, and the seal of the living God can be fixed upon that character. [Congregation: 'Amen.'] . . .

"Which would you rather have, the completeness, the perfect fullness, of Jesus Christ, or have less than that, with some of your sins covered up that you never know of? [Congregation: 'His fullness.'] . . . And so He has got to dig down to the deep places we never dreamed of, because we cannot understand our hearts. But the Lord knows the heart. He tries the conscience. He will cleanse the heart, and bring up the last vestige of wickedness. Let Him go on, brethren; let Him keep on His searching work. And when He does bring our sins before us, let the heart say, 'Lord, Thou gavest Thyself for my sins. Oh, I take Thee instead of them.' They are gone, and I rejoice in the Lord. Brethren, let us be honest with the Lord, and treat Him as He wants us to" (A. T. Jones, *1893 General Conference Bulletin*, pp. 404-405).

Scripture calls this process of enlightenment and cleansing *judgment*. Carefully notice Isaiah's usage of the word:

"And it shall come to pass that he who is left in Zion and remains in Jerusalem will be called holy—everyone who is recorded among the living in Jerusalem. When the Lord has washed away the filth of the daughters of Zion, and purged the blood of Jerusalem from her midst, by the spirit of judgment and by the spirit of burning . . ." (Isaiah 4:3-4).

We generally think of judgment as a negative thing that only happens to the wicked. But here the Bible speaks of judgment as a positive thing that occurs in the spiritual experience of believers. For those who follow on to know the Lord there will be washing from moral filth. Isaiah says that the means by which this cleansing will occur is "the spirit of judgment and . . . burning." What is meant by this idea of sin being removed by judgment?

The word *judgment* simply means "discernment" or "perception." A judge is someone who discerns between right and wrong and discloses his perception. He discovers the truth and makes it known. When we say, "That woman has good judgment," we mean she has a keen sense of discernment. What the Bible calls "the day of judgment" (Matthew 10:15, 12:36; 1 John 4:17) is the time when every mind will be brought to perfect awareness in the blazing light of God's perfect discernment of all things.

"Each one's work will become clear; for the Day [of judgment] will declare it, because it will be revealed by fire; and the fire will test each one's work, of what sort it is" (1 Corinthians 3:13).

"Therefore judge nothing before the time, until the Lord comes, who will both bring to light the hidden things of darkness and reveal the counsels of the hearts" (1 Corinthians 4:5).

The biblical idea of judgment is that all human beings, believers and unbelievers alike, are destined for perfect self-awareness in the light of God's absolute holiness.

"Some men's sins are open beforehand, going before to judgment; and some men they follow after. Likewise also the good works of some are manifest beforehand; and they that are otherwise cannot be hid" (1 Timothy 5:24-25, KJV).

Those who are finally saved and those who are finally lost are brought to view in this Scripture. Both experience "judgment." The difference lies in how and when they deal with their sins. Those who are finally saved choose to have their sins "open" to their awareness "beforehand." In this life they allow "the judgment" to transpire in their hearts as an enlightening and cleansing experience. They consistently merge toward the light of God's love and righteousness and truth. Knowing Him leads them to know themselves in contrast. With each step closer to God they say *yes* to His love and *no* to their sins. In this way their sins have been judged and cleansed, discerned and given up.

The eternally lost will face their final judgment when they stand in God's unveiled presence. Paul says the opening of their sins will "follow after" and "cannot be hid." By this statement he means that their sins will be fully opened to their consciousness on the final Day of Judgment, whereas the saved have allowed their sins to be exposed beforehand. On that day of final and full reckoning, the lost will know perfectly "the judgment [discernment] of God" and will sink into unavoidable "indignation and wrath, tribulation and anguish" of "soul [psyche]" (Romans 2:3, 8-9). Having persistently chosen to retain their sins and reject God's merciful, cleansing love, their hearts are filled with unresolved guilt. In the light of God's perfect righteousness and His just hatred of sin, the wicked will see and feel their guilt with undimmed clarity. The choice is before us: judgment now or judgment later, but all will see as they are seen and know as they are known.

I should have known God's love would be invasive. How could it be otherwise? Such is the nature of love. It wants to both know and be known. Did I foolishly imagine that the Lover of my soul would be content to keep our relationship shallow—familiar enough to be called an acquaintance, but distant enough to keep us strangers? Did I somehow contrive that He would settle for stimulating my intellect and playing with my emotions—a mere recreational religion—but never pry deeply into my soul?

If such have been my imaginings, I must cast them aside at once. The husband of my wayward heart would have all of me or none at all. But I shrink back as I contemplate the price of total honesty and unreserved commitment. Should I get that real with God? Just thinking about it, I can nearly feel the heat on my heart. And I know that if I allow complete contact, parts of me will begin to melt away and finally burn to ashes. Will there be anything left of the only me I know? I vacillate in the tension of my freedom.

But then, as I look upon Jesus in His selfless love, a realization grips me. Whatever parts of me would consume away in the flame of His loving penetration into my heart are parts not worth retaining. And yes, there would be something left. The true self He meant me to be would emerge from the fire free from all pretense, deceit and false sense of self. So I ask myself, "Why should I be as one who veils herself?" (Song of Solomon 1:7). "I am my beloved's, and his desire is toward me" (7:10). He means me no harm, but only the blessing of complete restoration to Himself.

My decision is made. I choose to live my life before the mirror of His character. By making that choice I have also chosen to face everything in me contrary to His holy love. I expect there will be pain at times, but only the pain of escape from my old self into the pleasure of deeper intimacy with Him whom my soul loves.

With my decision made, I pray:

"Let me see Your face,

Let me hear Your voice;

For Your voice is sweet,

And Your face is lovely" (Song of Solomon 2:14).

— *Chapter Eighteen* —

Falling in Love
Long Distance
SANCTIFICATION

Know His heart,
    Feel His mind,
Probe His depths,
    And you will find,
Such beauty of person,
    All else above,
You'll die to fear,
    And awake to love.

CONRAD AND PORCIA fell in love long distance. He lived on the East Coast, she on the West Coast. They met on the Internet in a Christian chat room. From there they "stepped" out of the room and began chatting alone with one another, first once or twice a week, then every day, and finally upon waking, on breaks at work, and before going to bed each night.

As the weeks and months passed, casual acquaintance shifted to friendship. They talked about everything. Their likes and dislikes, their families, their work, their goals in life and their spiritual values. They even discussed the kind of person each of them would like to marry some day. And to their surprise and delight, they found they were describing one another.

"It seems to me," Conrad typed one evening, "that you are the kind of person I want to marry."

Although she was startled by those abrupt words, Porcia could not help but respond the way she did.

"I feel the same way about you, Conrad."

And so, the Internet friendship shifted gears into an Internet romance. The chats became more and more personal. Conrad and Porcia were entering the sacred realm of one another's heart, endearing themselves to one another by exposing their inner thoughts and feelings, attended by expressions of care and affection. They were falling in love.

But there was a problem. They had never met in person. Neither of them had any idea what the other looked like. The prospect was a bit unnerving, especially for Conrad. One day a friend of Conrad's, who was up to date on the long-distance romance, razzed him:

"OK, Lover Boy, so you're in love with a lady you've never met?"

"No," Conrad reacted, "that's not entirely true. I have met her, in a sense. I know everything about this woman. She's the greatest person I've ever known."

"Nearly everything," his friend retorted. "You have no idea what she looks like. For all you know she could be the twin sister of Lassie."

As much as Conrad hated to admit it, his friend was right. But the fact remained, he was in love with Porcia. His decision was made. He would pop the big question.

Sitting at the keyboard one evening, as one of their chat sessions was about to close for some much-needed sleep, Conrad began to type:

"Porcia, will you ma . . ."

He paused. He struggled. He perspired.

"Will you ma . . ."

As much as he wanted to, he couldn't type those final two words . . . *marry me*. Suddenly he lost control of his fingers as his friend's words echoed in his mind, "She could be the twin sister of Lassie."

Before he could think twice, he typed the words, "Will you mail me a photo of yourself?"

Nearly every guy reading this story is thinking, "Whoa, buddy, that was a close call! Good thinking. You did the right thing."

Nearly every woman reading this story is thinking, "What a shallow jerk!"

I don't know if Porcia was thinking the same thing, but this is what she typed in response:

"No, Conrad, please don't ask me to do that just yet. We need more time to get to know one another. I really want to know if you can love me for who I am in my heart. If you continue to love what you find in my personality and character, then I'll be happy to send a picture soon enough, and ask you to send one as well. And if we like what we see, then we can go from there."

Wow! This was almost more than Conrad could bear, but bear it he must. He knew *he* was good looking, but what about *her*?

"Why won't she send a picture?" he wondered aloud to himself. "Could the situation be tragic?"

Conrad had not yet learned that "beauty is in the eye of the beholder" and that "everyone is beautiful to someone."

Months passed by as he and Porcia continued to chat. Nothing changed for the worse. Both of them were more certain than ever of their mutual love. Photos were exchanged; they did like what they saw; Conrad popped the big question and Porcia said *yes*. When I met the happy couple, they had been married for six years. The only thing that surprised me was that Conrad bore a striking resemblance to Lassie, especially the nose. Oh, well. Beauty *is* in the eye of the beholder, fortunately for Porcia.

The story of Conrad and Porcia illustrates a vital truth we all need to understand: it is possible, perhaps even preferable, to fall in love long distance. This is especially true with God. But lots of people find it difficult to pursue a relationship with someone they can't see, hear or touch. And yet, the Bible expects us to do just that—to love God without seeing Him:

"Though you have never seen Him, yet you love Him. At present you trust Him without being able to see Him, and even now He brings you a joy that words cannot express and which has in it a hint of the glories of Heaven" (1 Peter 1:8, Phi).

Apparently, it is possible to have a love relationship with God without seeing Him, here in this present world. And that love, according to Peter, is a hint, a foretaste, of what Heaven will be all about.

At one of my seminars, a guy named Artie asked a question many people ask in one way or another:

"How am I supposed to know and love God if I can't see Him? Why does He maintain this distance? Why doesn't He just show up and interact with us in person? If He did, there probably wouldn't be one atheist in the world."

It's a good question. The first part of the answer isn't easy, for us or for God. As we noted in a previous chapter, the Lord told Moses, "You cannot see My face; for no man shall see Me, and live" (Exodus 33: 20). This is not due to any hostility on God's part, but rather due to our sinfulness, which makes it impossible for us to have immediate contact with Him and survive. The clashing contrast between God's love and our self-centeredness must be removed before we can endure face-to-face fellowship with Him.

The second part of the answer is better news. God *has* revealed Himself by means of "email," so to speak, in His Word. And He *has* shown up on earth in person, in Christ, and the record of His life is also contained in the Holy Scriptures.

Porcia and Conrad fell in love by means of words on screen and paper, because by words the heart and mind are communicated. A letter says far more about a person than the color of their eyes or the length of their hair or any other physical features. God has given us His Word. In it we encounter His thoughts and feelings and the history of His actions in dealing with the human race. The Bible unfolds the character of God. I think God is doing something similar to what Porcia did with Conrad. By giving us His Word and asking us to know Him through it, He seems to be saying, "If you can fall in love with Me for who I am at heart, if you find My character attractive, then you will meet Me soon enough face to face."

This really is the best way for God to introduce Himself to us, even though we may think we would prefer a different method. The written word of Scripture is a creation of divine genius in motion—a living, active, communicating medium that effectively unfolds God's identity. The necessity of approaching Him through a written revelation drives us in the direction of deeply pondering His character, allowing us to respond unforced by the overpowering influence of His visible majesty. By giving us the Bible, God has shown Himself to be a gentleman, respectfully preserving our freedom to think through His claims and say *yes* or *no* without coercion. If He were to follow the advice of Artie and simply show up at our doorstep, so to speak, we would be overwhelmed by the event. In our fallen condition we would tremble with terror in His holy presence, not because He is scary, but because we would be scared. I suppose every person on earth would "believe" and vow "obedience," if anyone were still alive. Atheism would vanish overnight, the whole world would get baptized and we'd all be "religious." And yet, the most vital question would remain unanswered, suspended as an echoing, haunting dirge amid all the religious activity:

"Does anyone know and love God?"

Sure, He could make us slaves in an instant with a razzle-dazzle approach, but He couldn't make us His intelligent, love-motivated friends. A man doesn't usually ask a woman to marry him with a gun pointed at her head. Why not? Seems like that would be a pretty effective method. Well, it depends on what a guy wants. Is he seeking love or control? If love, then the pistol approach won't work. For the same reason, God refuses to extend to us His proposal of eternal marriage by the sheer force of His glorious presence. He is aiming for something more, far more, than control. God desires our friendship, based on freewill love and trust.

In the light of this divine purpose, a very practical question presents itself. How can we effectively use the Bible as a channel through which we allow God to communicate with us? How can we handle the written revelation of Scripture in such a way that it will escort our hearts into an ever-deepening love for Him? To address this important matter is the aim of the next chapter.

— *Chapter Nineteen* —

Divine–Human Fellowship
DISCIPLINE

Punch the pedal,
    Merge left, speed by;
Crank the wheel right,
    Get vertical and fly.
Radical devotion,
    To God evermore;
Extreme, no danger,
    In His love to soar.

Let's get practical. In this chapter I want to show you *how* to fall in love and stay in love with God long distance, preparatory to meeting Him face to face without fear. From the story of Conrad and Porcia we learned that true love for God is awakened in us and deepens as we become intimately acquainted with His character. In the previous chapter we concluded that the Bible is the primary medium through which God has chosen to reveal His character to us. Now let's allow John and Paul to get more specific with us. First John speaks:

"That which was from the beginning, which we have heard, which we have seen with our eyes, which we have looked upon, and our hands have handled, concerning the Word of life—the life was manifested, and we have seen, and bear witness, and declare to you that eternal life which was with the Father and was manifested to us—that which we have seen and heard we declare to you, that you also may have fellowship with us; and truly our fellowship is with the Father and with His Son Jesus Christ. And these things we write to you that your joy may be full" (1 John 1:1-4).

What an incredible testimony! Did you catch what John is saying here? We can almost hear the excitement in his voice. *The very Word*, he explains, *that was from the beginning; the very Life that has existed with the Father in eternal ages past, stepped right out of eternity into our immediate presence. We interacted with that Word, that Life, in person. We saw Him with our own eyes, heard Him speak with our own ears, and literally touched Him with our hands. We had a personal, visible, audible encounter with God veiled in human flesh!*

Why is John telling us this?

His stated goal is to draw us into personal fellowship with himself and the others who met God in Christ, and through their testimony to escort us into personal fellowship with the Father and with His Son. The word here translated "fellowship" is *koinonia*. It has a richer meaning than the English word *fellowship* can express. Perhaps the most literal translation would be "communication" or "communion," meaning two-way interaction with the intent of achieving a mutual knowledge of one another's true and full person. God wants to communicate with us because He wants us to know Him. In turn, He wants us to open up our hearts to Him in complete and honest transparency. What an amazing calling!

"The Word" is God's chosen medium of fellowship or communication with us. John and the other apostle met the Word in the person of Jesus Christ. Their written testimony of His teachings, life, death and resurrection, constitutes the Word by which we may have fellowship with the Father and His Son.

This is such a high privilege. We have no idea how blessed we are to have the Word of God right in our laps. If "seen," "heard" and "handled" correctly, it will usher us into personal interaction with the God of the universe and open our hearts to a clear vision of His beautiful character of love.

According to the apostle Paul, our fellowship with God through His word involves a vital discipline he calls "beholding." Notice:

"We all, with unveiled face, beholding as in a mirror the glory of the Lord, are being transformed into the same image from glory to glory, just as by the Spirit of the Lord" (2 Corinthians 3:18).

In the context of this verse, Paul points out that the veil here spoken of is a mental and emotional veil: "A veil lies on their heart" (verse 15). That which the veil hides is "the glory of the Lord," which is a biblical word for the character of God (Exodus 33:18-19). Paul's key point is that "the veil is taken away in Christ" (2 Corinthians 3:14). In other words, God's character is clearly revealed to us in the life and death of Jesus. Paul elaborates:

"For it is God who commanded light to shine out of darkness, who has shone in our hearts to give the light of the knowledge of the glory [character] of God in the face of Jesus Christ" (2 Corinthians 4:6).

Jesus is "the radiant revelation of God's character and the exact image of His person" (Hebrews 1:3, personal translation). There is only one way for the veil of darkness to be removed from our minds: by "beholding" all that God has revealed of Himself in Christ. Otherwise, the veil will remain. We will not know God as He really is, and we will not find it possible in our hearts to love Him.

What, then, does it mean to engage in this thing the Bible calls "beholding"? How does one do it?

It is not anything mystical, but rather very practical, calling upon us to give some time and energy. What we've been doing in this book, chapter by chapter, is an example of *beholding* the character of God. We have been engaging the focused attention of our minds and hearts on various aspects of who God is, what He's like, how He thinks and feels. By doing this, we come to know Him. Gradually, with each additional penetration of light into our minds, the darkness of misconception about Him is dispelled. As we come to know Him, we are continually faced with the choice to believe or disbelieve the truth, to say *yes* or *no* to the light. If we say *yes*, then we grow in our love for Him.

Most of those who read this book will do so by what we might call *casual beholding*. There's nothing wrong with *casual beholding*. In fact, we need to do lots of it, filling up as much of our leisure time as possible with keeping God's character before us by simply reading, reading, reading the Bible and other books that attempt to unfold His heart. But *casual beholding* is not all we need.

Moving a step closer in our fellowship with God, we may engage in what we might call *meditative beholding*.

Take a passage of Scripture, ask God to communicate with you, and then read it slowly, two, three, even four or five times. Once the passage is read in your main version of choice—preferably a more literal translation like the King James, New King James or the New American Standard Version—to the point that the basic message is before your mind, then read it again in a few other translations and paraphrases: The New International Version, Today's English Version, The Message, The Amplified Bible, etc. Now you are beginning to catch the tone and feelings of the passage and notice details and nuances that enlarge your understanding. Pause to think, to feel, to imagine the picture Scripture paints. Pause to pray, "God, what do You want me to see here?" Meditatively read sections from the life of Christ, especially the closing scenes leading up to the cross. Let your imagination try to grasp and see every action of the Savior and every interaction with Him.

Then there is what we might call *intensive beholding*. While reading this book may be an example of *casual* or even *meditative* beholding, writing this book required a more focused, prayerful, intentional probing for the meaning of God's Word, for answers to significant questions and, most of all, for clearer perception of God's character. *Intensive beholding* requires sustained periods of thought and concentration on a given passage, and then recording on paper what we see.

I'm not talking about writing books, but simply writing. My primary reason for writing is not to be an author. In fact, I began writing with no intention of getting published. Even if nothing I write would ever be in print for others to read, I'd still spend my whole life writing.

Why?

Because I know of no better way to experience significant growth in the knowledge of God. In my opinion, beholding God's character is the single most productive discipline in which the Christian can engage, and writing is the second most vital discipline. Writing turns up the volume on beholding, allowing us to hear far more than we otherwise could. The process of recording our thoughts on paper has a way of clarifying what we believe, revealing inconsistencies in our thinking and pressing us to see beyond the surface to "the deep things of God" (1 Corinthians 2:10). Writing takes on the form of communication with God far more effectively than thought prayer or even audible prayer. Writing also communicates to us. As you go back and read what you have written, you will be amazed at what you were thinking. Finally, writing prepares us to more effectively communicate with others as we have occasion to speak on our God's behalf.

I realize this may sound like work. There is no doubt that to do what I'm suggesting will require some energy and effort. But I assure you, if you take up the habit of *recording* what you *behold,* the intellectual, emotional and spiritual rewards will be well worth the effort.

And yet, let me put your mind at ease, to some degree at least. Writing is not as hard as most people think, if you don't attempt to produce literature or genius or poetry or prose. Just write. Forget about correcting your grammar and spelling. Forget about trying to write something for the bestseller list. Forget about trying to write something even burglars might read some day. Just write.

Here's how you can get started:

1. First, decide to do it. Make a conscious decision to record your thoughts and feelings and questions about God.

2. Purchase a pile of notepads, bound notebooks or completely blank journals. Write the date on the first notebook and put it with your Bible.

3. On the first page, write something like this: *God, I want to know You*

*more than anything else. Please communicate with me as I engage my mind
in the discipline of beholding Your character and writing down what I learn.
Thank You, in Jesus, Amen.*

4. On the second page, write *Ephesians 2:8-10* at the top. Turn to the
passage and read it slowly, underlining the words and phrases that stand out
and catch your attention.

"For by <u>grace</u> you have been <u>saved</u> through <u>faith</u>, and that not of
yourselves; it is the gift of God, not of works, lest anyone should boast. For
we are His <u>workmanship</u>, created in Christ Jesus for good works, which God
prepared beforehand that we should walk in them."

5. Under *Ephesians 2:8-10* write, "What is the meaning of this Scripture?"

6. Do what we described earlier as meditative beholding.

7. Using a dictionary and a *Strong's Concordance,* look up the underlined
words and write any definitions that increase your understanding of the text.

<u>Grace</u>: "*Charis* (which, by the way, is the Greek word from which I
derived the name *Charisa* in the chapter, *Concealed to Reveal*), graciousness .
. . the divine influence upon the heart and its reflection in the life" (*Strong's
Concordance*).

"Beauty or charm of form, movement, or expression. Goodwill; favor; the
love and favor of God toward man" (*Webster's*).

"The free, unmerited love and favor of God" (*Webster's 1828 Dictionary*).

<u>Saved</u>: "*Sozo,* to deliver, heal, make whole" (*Strong's*).

"To deliver from sin" (*Webster's*).

<u>Faith</u>: "*Pistis,* persuasion, credence, conviction (of truth) . . . truth itself
. . . assurance, belief" (*Strong's*).

"Complete trust" (*Webster's*).

<u>Workmanship</u>: "*Poiema,* a product . . . thing that is made," from which
we get the English word "poem." (*Strong's*).

Always pay attention to conjunctions: *and, but, if, through, therefore,
which,* etc. These words are important because they connect concepts and
words, showing their relation to one another. For example, having noted the
conjunctions in our text, you might write in your notebook:

Grace is the primary means *by* which I'm saved, while faith is the
secondary channel *through* which I receive grace. And while I'm not saved by
means *of* works, I am saved *for* the production of good works.

8. After pursuing the meaning of the text, write out your own amplified

version, incorporating what you have learned. You might write something like this:

"By means of God's totally undeserved love and favor toward me, I am delivered from the guilt and power of sin, through believing and trusting in the truth of that unearnable love. Salvation, and even the ability to believe in His saving love, is a gift from God, not produced by my effort or earned by my right doing; for if I could contribute anything to my salvation, I'd take the glory and credit to myself. The truth is, by His unearnable love He shapes my life into a poetic masterpiece of virtuous living, all created in the person of Jesus before I even believed."

By writing out an enlarged paraphrase of the text, you have recorded and solidified your understanding.

9. Finally, write whatever. Prayers. Questions. Further observations about the text. Whatever comes to mind.

By forming the habit of beholding God's character and writing out what you learn, you will arrive at a personal understanding of Scripture.

A note of caution: while it is true that God will lead our minds as we make them available to Him, we are not prophets. He is able to guide our thinking to the degree that we are open and prepared to understand. Because of our liabilities as sinners, and because we are engaged in a growth process, every idea that comes into our heads and gets onto paper will not necessarily be totally clear, accurate or even true. So always hold your personal understanding with humility, and remain open for God to correct you through further study or through another person. Be open to how God is leading others and what they have to contribute. I've heard some people say, "I only read God's Word, never any books written by non-inspired authors." Such persons will sooner or later either be stunted in their spiritual growth or develop their very own personal brand of heresy. If they do read only the Bible, they obviously haven't read much of it. For if they had, they would have come to the part in the Bible that tells them to be learners of the teachings of others in the body of Christ. For God has given "gifts to men . . . some to be apostles, some prophets, some evangelists, and some pastors and teachers [obviously to speak and write], for the equipping of the saints for the work of ministry, for the edifying of the body of Christ, till we all come to the unity of the faith and of the knowledge of the Son of God, to a perfect man, to the measure of the stature of the fullness of

Christ" (Ephesians 4:8-13). There are gifted thinkers and communicators who speak and write things that will be very helpful to us. Tapping into this giftedness will help us grow more rapidly and more balanced as we listen and read. So don't be reluctant to read widely. You are not obligated to swallow everything anyone teaches, but you can glean much from what God is doing with other people's minds. Just hold fast to that which is good, and chuck the rest.

Beholding the beauty of God's character, whether you use the approach I've suggested here or some other method more to your liking, is the single most important part of your life. Your job is not more important. Your human relationships are not more important. Brushing your teeth and taking showers are not more important (but please don't stop). Not even eating, drinking and breathing are more important. All of these things are crucial, but fellowship with God is a matter more crucial than all else, for every other aspect of your life will be shaped and directed by your relationship with God and how you see His character.

As you "behold what manner of love the Father has bestowed on us" (1 John 3:1), John promised that "your joy [will] be full" (1 John 1:4). Knowing and loving God increases the quality of your life. It sharpens the colors and details of all you see and experience, enlarging your capacity for happiness, deepening your sense of meaning and satisfaction, even when life demands that you struggle and cry.

If you will begin a long-distance relationship with God via "email"— pondering His written word to you and communicating (perhaps even on paper) your thoughts, feelings, questions and prayers to Him—I guarantee you, by the authority of Scripture, you will fall in love with Him. How could you not, for He is "altogether lovely" and beautiful beyond compare.

— *Chapter Twenty* —

Love Counts the Days
ADVENT

"I am my beloved's,
And His desire is toward me."

Song of Solomon 7:10

HEARTS THAT ARE in love can't stand to be separated. Lover and beloved must find the fastest way to be together, and until that day there is a distinct longing hovering over their lonely hearts. They watch time tick by with an ever-present consciousness of the space between them.

I know these feelings well. For the past twenty years my life has been a nonstop series of appointments and deadlines that take me far from home. And to be far from home has nothing to do with being far from a house. It means to be far from that female heart that is one with my own.

The church is to God a female heart. One of the delightful mysteries of the Christian faith is that the God we worship is a Lover at heart, who regards His church as a beloved bride and not as a servile subject.

"Husbands, love your wives, just as Christ also loved the church and gave Himself for her, that He might sanctify and cleanse her with the washing of water by the word, that He might present her to Himself a glorious church, not having spot or wrinkle or any such thing, but that she should be holy and without blemish. . . . For we are members of His body, of His flesh and His bones. 'For this reason a man shall leave his father and mother and be joined to his wife, and the two shall become one flesh.' This is a great mystery, but I speak concerning Christ and the church" (Ephesians 5:25-27, 30-32).

"A great mystery," indeed!

It is truly astounding that we, mere created beings and fallen at that, should be so deeply loved by God that He would condescend to make us "one flesh" with Himself. That the God of the universe would desire us to be His bride, forever united to Him in the closest bonds of intimacy, is almost unbelievable. And we wouldn't believe it had not Christ given the totality of Himself on the cross to prove it true.

There are levels of intensity to love's longing, increasing with the passage of time. If I'm gone from Sue's presence for only a weekend, I merely think about her and call home along the way. My work easily preoccupies my mind. If I'm gone for a whole week, I start to imagine what she's doing as she awakens to each new day, and every beautiful thing I see reminds me of her. If I'm gone for an entire month, watch out! I start to write poetry about her and trace my memories of the life we have shared. My mind's eye can see her. I hear her voice and smell her scent. I hate to admit it, but I even start to pout. And as time rolls by, its quality low and its pace slow in her absence, I begin to count the days, wondering if there might be some way to hasten our reuniting.

Turn now to another parting. Recreate in your heart the high-pitched emotion of a separation too big for words. Imagine the intense feelings that charge the air as the Savior says goodbye to His disciples and promises to return, for they are also your own feelings if He has captured your heart with His love.

There He stands with tentative posture, not at all eager to announce His departure. He is sad and excited at the same time. Sad because He must leave our world, disappear from our sight and fade from our hearing. Excited because He longs to see His Father and the Holy Spirit, not to mention His beloved angel friends. With part of His heart He doesn't want to leave, and yet He must, if we are to ever be fully and forever reunited with Him. So He gently breaks the news, giving the assurance that the separation won't last forever:

"Let not your heart be troubled; you believe in God, believe also in Me. In My Father's house are many mansions; if it were not so, I would have told you. I go to prepare a place for you. And if I go and prepare a place for you, I will come again and receive you to Myself; that where I am, there you may be also" (John 14:1-3).

Can you see the looks of bewilderment and disappointment on the faces of the disciples?

"Going away? Where? Why? Please don't leave!"

There is no sense of materialistic concern in these words of Jesus. The word *mansions* in the King James Version is not the best translation. The Greek word simply means *places*, or "rooms," as rendered in the New International Version. I'm not suggesting that we won't have mansions. But I really don't see the point of caring whether we will or not. Certainly everything will be "mansion" level in that place. However, the idea Jesus has in mind is not material luxury, but togetherness. The Father wants us to live with Him, to be forever close to Him. Jesus wants the same. As family members share a house, so we are invited to have a place in God's house, in His presence, at His table, in His company.

Being far from home has nothing to do with being far from a house, no matter how posh the heavenly pad will be. To be far from home means to be far from the ones who live there, to be far from God our Father, from Jesus and from the Holy Spirit.

Streets of gold, gates of pearl, a city mansion and a country house—all these things are going to be great, but they're not what going to Heaven is all about. It's all about love. It's about the longing heart of the divine Lover meeting the longing heart of His beloved human bride, and finding eternal ecstasy in one another's friendship.

According to Jesus, our destiny is a *person* more than a *place*, for the place only has meaning due to the presence of that Person. With the words, "to the Father," Jesus explained where He is leading us. The Father is our destiny, not Heaven per se. The religion of the Bible is deeply personal. Its whole tenor is oriented toward relational connectivity between each individual human person with God the person.

While we pour our energies into debating over "the *manner* of Christ's second coming," an aching vacancy yawns wide in God's heart; and as we proof-text the world to death, that yearning divine heart is kept hidden from their view, and from our own.

- Secret Rapture vs. Visible Coming
- Pre-tribulation vs. Post-tribulation
- "Left Behind" vs. "Taken Up"

It is important to know *how* He will return; but it is deadly to the heart of our religion and our witness to the world to so focus in that direction that we fail to emphasize *why* He's coming back. Jesus is returning to earth because He loves us with an unquenchable, everlasting love which will not rest until we are with Him. Scripture presents the Second Coming primarily as a stimulus of longing and hope for God's presence, not merely as an argumentative discourse on how Jesus will return. The manner of His coming can and should be presented in such a way as to communicate the real heart of the matter: "I will come again and receive you to Myself, that where I am there you may be also." Looking forward to His second coming, Jesus prayed, "Father, I desire that they also whom You gave Me may be with Me where I am . . . that the love with which You have loved Me may be in them and I in them" (John 17:24, 26).

What if we were to proclaim and introduce such a God as this to our lonely, hurting world? What if we were to tell them that God longs for their eternal companionship with a love stronger than death, a love that does not regard even Heaven itself a place to be desired as long as we are lost?

Sure, we can argue that the "secret" rapture is a false teaching, but what solid ground have we really gained in the hearts of our hearers? The "non-secret" rapture is also false when presented void of its true meaning in Christ. Any Bible truth becomes false when reduced to an intellectual argument emptied of the gospel of God's love. If the idea that a true doctrine can be made false by detachment from Christ is too strong for your taste, you must at least agree that it would be pointless and void of saving power. It would be so powerful if we, the Church, were to make an intentional, concerted effort to communicate the Second Coming, and every other Bible doctrine, in the immediate context of God's love, and as a demonstration of God's love.

"For the Lord Himself will descend from heaven with a shout, with the voice of an archangel, and with the trumpet of God. And the dead in Christ will rise first. Then we who are alive and remain shall be caught up together with them in the clouds to meet the Lord in the air. And thus we shall always be with the Lord. Therefore comfort one another with these words" (1 Thessalonians 4:16-18).

While we've trained our minds to notice "the shout" and the "trumpet" in this passage so we can prove that the "rapture" will be no "secret," we often miss Paul's actual point. The noise of the Second Coming is merely incidental to meeting and being with the Lord. Paul wants his readers to imagine meeting the Lord Jesus Christ face to face, heart to heart.

Sight. As He draws near in a cloud of angels, closer and closer, soon His visible person will take on shape before our eyes. Our hearts will begin to race with excitement. Closer He will descend until we begin to make out His facial features with our eyes squinted. Closer still He will come. Our gaze will relax into perfect sight until we find ourselves just inches from Him. In His eyes we will read unreserved acceptance. His body language will communicate His earnest desire for us to be comfortable in His presence.

Hearing. He will speak, and we will hear the audible voice of God the Son. What will it sound like? What will He say? We have no way of knowing the exact first words we will hear from His lips, but we can be absolutely certain they will be words filled with enthusiastic reception. Perhaps something like, "I am so very happy you are here with Me."

Touch. And then, can you imagine reaching out your hands to literally touch the incarnate, glorified God? Or most likely, He will reach out to touch each of us first. His hand on your shoulder, on your cheek. Your head pressed to His chest with your arms wrapped around Him, and His arms engulfing you. His lips pressed gently to your face to kiss away tears of pain and draw forth tears of joy! Our bodies will tremble and then relax at His touch.

"We," you and I, dear friend, will actually "meet" the Lord Jesus Christ, God the Father and the Holy Spirit. We will feel perfectly loved before their approving gaze, perfectly affirmed by their words, and perfectly received by their touch. And from that day onward, into the far reaches of eternity future, "thus we shall always be with the Lord." There is absolutely nothing this world has to offer that can in the slightest degree compare with the prospect of meeting the Creator of the universe at His second coming. And so we call out to the heavens, "Come, Lord Jesus!"

Hearts that are in love can't stand to be separated. He longs to be with you. Do you feel the same toward Him? If you do, you will likely find yourself thinking about Him every day. Every beautiful thing you see will remind you of Him. You may even burst forth into poetry or song occasionally to express your affection and adoration. And without question, you will view the passing of time as bringing you nearer to His glorious return. You will count the days, wondering if there might be some way of "hastening" His coming (2 Peter 3:12).

— Chapter Twenty-One —

"Pleasures Forevermore"

HEAVEN

Pleasure once conceived by God
In holy waves of light,
Morphed by sin to demigod,
Passion's parasite.
Then came One with passions our own,
All pleasures to redeem;
In Him all joys are now regrown,
To thwart the hijack scheme.

THE DAY AFTER one of the longest and most sleepy church services
ever to occur on Planet Earth, my son and I were standing at the top of
a beautiful snow-covered mountain. The view was so spectacular! The air
was fresh and crisp, flooding our lungs and energizing our bodies for the
adventure before us. As we adjusted our gloves and goggles, preparing to
nearly fly down the ski run, Jason looked at me and asked a serious question
which was weighing on his teenage heart:

"Dad, it's so beautiful up here and so exhilarating . . ."

A pause of silence.

"Dad, is Heaven gonna be like the longest church service in history?"

I think a lot of people would ask the same question, if they thought
they could do so without appearing too unspiritual. Fact is, religious services
can easily descend into impersonal, mechanical forms that threaten to put
us fast to sleep "in God's presence." Religion itself, while inviting people to
Heaven, may be conducted in such a manner as to give a false impression of
what Heaven will be like.

King David anticipated the farthest possible extreme opposite to sleep
and boredom in God's presence:

"In Your presence is fullness of joy; at Your right hand are pleasures
forevermore" (Psalm 16:11).

Hmm.

Pleasure.

Now there's a charged word, especially for religious folk. But it is
definitely a biblical word, and one that describes what the redeemed will
forever experience in God's presence.

Originally the Creator placed humanity in the Garden of Eden, which
means Garden of *Pleasure*. God designed Adam and Eve with eyes to see,
ears to hear, tongues to taste, noses to smell, skin to touch, minds to explore

and emotions to feel. Our physiological and psychological make-up clearly indicate that our Designer engineered us for pleasure. It was never His plan that human beings should experience any kind of pain, dissatisfaction or even discomfort. In mind and body we were crafted to forever soar with perfect sensory ecstasy. By means of the plan of salvation God intends to completely restore all true delights to Edenic purity.

But pleasure can be a tricky thing, as you have no doubt noticed. It is, in fact, quite difficult to manage due to the introduction of sin into our psyche. Allow me a few moments of your time to explain what pleasure is, how it lives and how it dies.

Pleasure *given* is love. But pleasure *taken* is selfishness, which is the essence of sin. Grab for it, and pleasure won't build like a reservoir, but rather leak like a funnel. When given, pleasure is something added—there is more of life. When pleasure is taken, it is something consumed—there is less of life. Pleasure was designed by the Creator as an experiential phenomenon to be ministered upon the individual self by others, not by self upon self. To be given, never gotten, is the law of pleasure. The moment pleasure is chased as a primary objective for pleasure's sake, as though it were an end in itself, it eludes our grasp and leaves us more empty than before. Immediately, the law of diminishing returns kicks into motion and life begins to ebb away. The more we take, the less we have, until at last we are completely bankrupt of even the ability to experience pleasure at all. Our capacity for pleasure is blunted by self-indulgence, but enlivened by forgetting self and ministering to the joy of others.

Are there pleasures to be had from sin? Yes, most definitely. But Scripture calls them "the passing pleasures of sin" (Hebrews 11:25). *Passing* means "temporary, short-term, fading." On the other hand, the "pleasures" received in God's presence last "forevermore" (Psalm 16:11). In a sense, sin possesses no inherent pleasure at all. The pleasure derived from sin is hijacked, riding illicitly on the back of the good things God has made for our enjoyment. Sin is a parasite attached to God's natural order. Pleasure does not belong to sin. It belongs to God and His kingdom. Every slight ripple and massive explosion of pleasure you have ever experienced was but a faint hint of the ecstasy that awaits those who cross the threshold into eternity to live in God's love.

Sometimes God is accused of being a party pooper and a killjoy because His law warns us not to sin on pain of death. But when God says, "the wages of sin is death" (Romans 6:23), He does not mean, "If you sin I'll kill you, because I don't want you having any fun." He means, "Sin will destroy you and I want you to live so you can experience the endless pleasures I have in store for you."

When seen properly, God's law is the only real context in which true and lasting pleasure can exist. It is not a restrictive list of rules intended to forbid happiness, but rather a "law of liberty" (James 2:12) designed to impart and protect eternal joys. King David had the right idea when He sang to God, "I run the course of Your commandments, for You shall enlarge my heart" (Psalm 119:32). The NIV renders the last part of this verse, "for You have set my heart free." So far from being restrictive, God's law is extremely liberating. David sees a vast horizon of freedom within God's commandments, with plenty of room to "run." Those who obey the word of the Lord experience an enlargement of mental, emotional and physical capacity for happiness.

Sin, on the other hand, is very restrictive. "His own iniquities entrap the wicked man, and he is caught in the cords of his sin" (Proverbs 5:22). Sin blunts our finer sensibilities and shrinks our capacity for pleasure. It confines us as in a trap and ties our hands so that we can't move freely.

Jesus summarized the fundamental law of the universe with these words:

"Give, and it shall be given unto you; good measure, pressed down, and shaken together, and running over, shall men give into your bosom" (Luke 6:38, KJV).

It stands to reason that the opposite is also true:

Take, and it shall be taken from you; less and less you will have, until there is nothing left.

"There is one who makes himself rich, yet has nothing; and one who makes himself poor, yet has great riches" (Proverbs 13:7).

Love, by intrinsic composition, is reciprocal or, we might say, creative, which means it is focused out of itself. Love produces in its own likeness by arousing a selfless response in its object. Because love expends self for others, the others stand in spontaneous gratitude and experience a responsive sense of glad indebtedness. The recipient of love's selfless pleasure is made full to overflowing with life and vitality. Psychological and emotional enrichment spring up in the soul, creating the desire to give love in return. Thus the circle of love and life is made complete.

From our fallen perspective love appears to be totally upside down and backwards, when in fact it is completely right side up and forward. We don't get it. To us love is scary because it doesn't look like it will *work*. But that is precisely the problem with our tweaked thinking—we always think in terms of whether it will *work*. And by *work* we mean pan out to our advantage, to the benefit of self. So, in actual fact, we don't want love. We want self-gratification, and we want to call it love. But love never operates with a calculating consciousness: "Let's see now, if I'm kind to that chap, chances are pretty good that he will be kind to me, and since he has something I want, I'll go ahead and give it a try." To the contrary, love doesn't measure returns. As Paul says, "Love . . . does not seek its own" (1 Corinthians 13:5).

All pleasure born of love occurs by the voluntary lessening of space between individual free persons as they reach out of themselves to bestow blessing on one another. The focus of each is upon the happiness of the others, with no concern for self. The space that lies between us is rightfully present due to our individuality and its inherent freedom. The removal of that space occurs when we choose to use our freedom to love others above ourselves.

Herein lies the secret of Heaven's eternal pleasures. All live for others and are forever empty. All live for others and are forever full. The definition of Heaven is this: free beings eternally engaging in the pleasure of God's perfect love, continually receiving love from Him as its primary source and in turn loving Him and all others with the same self-forgetful devotion. All the material benefits of Heaven—mansions of plenty and streets of gold—are incidental and peripheral to the pleasure of participating in God's love. And since the essence of Heaven's pleasure is to love and be loved, the quality of life we will experience there may begin here and now.

Scripture does not view eternal life as merely a future biological existence in the geographical location of Heaven. Rather, eternal life is an inner quality of life defined by intimacy with God, beginning in this present world and reaching into the new heavens and the new earth.

"This is eternal life, that they may know You, the only true God, and Jesus Christ whom You have sent" (John 17:3).

"God has given us eternal life, and this life is in His Son. He who has the Son has life; he who does not have the Son of God does not have life. These things I have written to you who believe in the name of the Son of

God, that you may know that you have eternal life" (1 John 5:11-13).

Eternal life is something we take to Heaven with us, not something we get when this life is over. We may know that we have eternal life here and now if we know the joy and peace of God's forgiving love. Every insight into the beauty of His character that thrills our souls, every sense of emotional satisfaction in His acceptance, every taste of His love we experience in this present world "has in it a hint of the glories of Heaven" (1 Peter 1:8, Phi). For the ultimate pleasure of Heaven will be intimacy with God.

"In my flesh I will see God; I myself will see Him with my own eyes— I, and not another. How my heart yearns within me! (Job 19:26-27, NIV).

Not that no one else will see Him, but I will see Him with such captivated love, and I will see such devoted love in Him for me, as though we are the only two hearts in all the universe. And the same will be true for you. You will see God with your own eyes, and not another. There is a sense in which you alone, exclusively, personally, will know His love. So shall I. There are two complementary realities that make this possible: God's infinitude and our individuality.

God's Infinitude. Hold a coin close to your eye. All you see is part of the coin. Pull it back a few inches and you can see the whole coin. Back up from your front door and you will see the height and width of your house. Back up far enough from the ground upon which you stand and you will see your continent. Farther still and you'll see the earth. Farther still and you'll see our galaxy. Back up far enough from anything and you will see that it has parameters. Everything has edges; everything has ends; everything, it turns out, is small. Everything, that is, except God's love. There is nowhere you can go in all the universe to be far from God's love. It has no bounds. No edges. No ends. No measurable height or depth. God's love is a circle whose center is everywhere and whose circumference is nowhere. It is an endless ocean of intricately beautiful contours, features and angles that the collective vision of all humans and angels could not even begin to see in totality. The steady focus of all the intellectual and emotional energy of all created beings for all eternity will never plumb its fathomless depths or scale its lofty heights. Each new discovery will only contribute to a multitude of previous discoveries to create the potential for a still more endless array of possible configurations and equations of insight. God's love is the only thing in the universe from which you can't back up far enough to take in the whole picture. It is infinite.

Our Individuality: The total distinctiveness of each human being is a wonder too high for comprehension. You are a completely unique person unlike any other. You have a capacity for thinking thoughts and feeling emotions and forming perspectives that are absolutely inaccessible to any other human being. In a very real sense, you alone see the world because no one else can see it just as you do. We all simultaneously see different aspects while looking at the same objects. Therefore, we all have something to share with others even as we occupy the same space. Truly there is no such thing as sameness, but only unity.

By virtue of these two immutable truths—God's infinitude and our individuality—we will each one forever experience a private intimacy with God. And He will know each of us like no other. Jesus has promised, "To him who overcomes I will give some of the hidden manna to eat. And I will give him a white stone, and on the stone a new name written which no one knows except him who receives it" (Revelation 2:17). The hidden manna represents undiscovered aspects of God's beautiful character, and we shall each receive and eat "some" from His hand of which no other can partake. The white stone with the new name, as a secret between each individual and God, symbolizes that the person we have become by His grace is known only to Him with nearest intimacy. Whatever your new, secret name will be, whenever He calls you to His side by that name, you will know that you are alone with Him in a special sense, sharing a love that is exclusively between you and Him.

David understood what Heaven is all about when he wrote, "One thing I have desired of the Lord, that will I seek: that I may dwell in the house of the Lord all the days of my life, to behold the beauty of the Lord, and to inquire in His temple" (Psalm 27:4).

The great joy of eternity will be the process of discovering new dimensions of the divine "beauty" and to "inquire" of God. Can you imagine having the mysteries of the universe opened to your understanding by God Himself? Can you imagine forever being in a constant state of fresh insight to divine beauties never before seen?

"How precious is Your lovingkindness, O God! Therefore the children of men put their trust under the shadow of Your wings. They are abundantly satisfied with the fullness of Your house, and You give them drink from the river of Your pleasures. For with You is the fountain of life; in Your light we see light" (Psalm 36:7-9).

Upon our arrival in Heaven, and as the numberless days go by in His company, what kind of person will we forever discover God to be? As with all questions about God the answer is in Jesus, Who is "the brightness of His glory and the express image of His person" (Hebrews 1:3).

In a beautiful display of selfless service, Jesus showed us the Father and revealed the spirit of Heaven. This magnificent unfolding of God's character occurred in the upper room where Jesus shared the Passover with His disciples.

The Savior was there, alone in the crowd. They had lost awareness of His presence. Each one was focused on backing up from all the others to preserve their false sense of self. Some were arguing, others were silent with rigid pride. The issue at hand was the menial task of foot washing.

As was the custom in that culture, when a gathering occurred in a home, dirty feet had to be washed. In many homes a servant would do the job. If no servant was present there was usually a natural, unspoken pecking order. Whoever occupied the lowest position on the social ladder was expected to perform the undesirable task. But what if a group got together that was made up of men who all viewed themselves as higher than all the others? Well, there would be some uncomfortable silence at least, and perhaps even some tense words calculated to apply pressure on someone to do the humiliating work. Or there may be a stubborn standoff, leaving everyone with dirty feet.

This was the situation in which Jesus found Himself with His disciples. They thought high was high and low was low. Reality was about to be redefined for them.

"Jesus . . . laid aside His garments, took a towel and girded Himself. After that, He poured water into a basin and began to wash the disciples' feet, and to wipe them with the towel with which He was girded" (John 13: 3-5).

"So when He had washed their feet, taken His garments, and sat down again, He said to them, 'Do you know what I have done to you? You call Me Teacher and Lord, and you say well, for so I am. If I then, your Lord and Teacher, have washed your feet, you also ought to wash one another's feet. For I have given you an example, that you should do as I have done to you. Most assuredly, I say to you, a servant is not greater than his Master" (John 13:12-16).

We can't help but ask, *Is this really God?* Do we dare answer *yes?* If we do, what are the implications? If the Creator of the universe regards serving the most menial needs of sinners to be equal to His dignity, what does that mean for us? Is there any act of service beneath our dignity?

We are inclined to make a distinction here between the humanity of Christ and His divinity. Surely He was merely *acting* the part of a servant, as the *human* Jesus, in order to teach us how we ought to be. Certainly the Almighty Creator of the universe is no servant, or so we think. But the Savior taught us to believe that what we witness in His life is a true and accurate revelation of the Father (John 14:9). When we see Jesus, the man, on His knees at the dirty feet of sinners, girded with a towel as a humble servant, we are witnessing the true character of the Father as well as that of the Son. God is a servant at heart—always has been, always will be. Jesus indicated that God will serve redeemed humanity in the kingdom to come:

"Blessed are those servants whom the Master, when He comes, will find watching. Assuredly, I say to you that He will gird Himself and have them sit down to eat, and will come and serve them" (Luke 12:37).

What an incredible picture!

Can you see it?

The great war between good and evil is over. Jesus has returned. The redeemed ascend into the clouds to meet Him. We pass through the gates into the City of God. Surrounded by the beauties of our new home, we are filled with a deep sense of unworthiness. The fact that He has even saved us is enough to bow us low with tears of awe and humility before Him. All we want to do is serve Him. But then God seats us at a table He has prepared especially for us. And rather than seating Himself at the head of the table to be served, our Creator will gird Himself and serve us. We, the ones who gave Him so much heartache, the ones who rebelled against His love and destroyed the world He gave us, the ones who poured out our rage and hatred on Him at the cross. Yes, you and me. God will gird Himself and serve us. He is a king with a servant's heart. This is the kind of person we will forever discover God to be.

What utter insanity it would be to even run the risk of not spending forever with this incredible God by refraining for another moment from saying *yes* to His invitation!

There lies before us an eternity of mind-expanding comprehension of God's character . . .

An eternity of ever-climaxing emotional ecstasy in His husbandly care . . .

An eternity of intimate friendship with the Creator of the universe . . .

There lies before us *An Endless Falling in Love.* It's "'time . . . to fall in love.' This is what the Sovereign Lord says."

Other books by Ty Gibson—

SEE WITH NEW EYES

SHADES OF GRACE

IN THE LIGHT OF GOD'S LOVE